RAND NATIONAL DEFENSE RESEARCH INSTITUTE

Recruiting Policies and Practices for Women in the Military

Views from the Field

Douglas Yeung, Christina E. Steiner, Chaitra M. Hardison, Lawrence M. Hanser, Kristy N. Kamarck

Prepared for the Office of the Undersecretary of Defense for Personnel and Readiness (OUSD/P&R)

For more information on this publication, visit www.rand.org/t/RR1538

Library of Congress Cataloging-in-Publication Data is available for this publication.
ISBN: 978-0-8330-9807-8

Published by the RAND Corporation, Santa Monica, Calif.

Preface

On January 24, 2013, then–Defense Secretary Leon E. Panetta announced an end to the ban on women in combat. As of January 1, 2016, the armed services have been required to implement efforts to provide equal opportunities regardless of gender. The public nature of this announcement has likely affected potential recruits' views of the military in as yet unknown ways. This research is intended to provide an early perspective on these effects and recommendations for how the services and the Office of the Under Secretary of Defense for Personnel and Readiness (OUSD/P&R) can adapt moving forward. RAND conducted this study to assist OUSD/P&R in identifying approaches for bolstering recruitment of women into the armed services during the years in which ground combat jobs are transitioning to include women. This report should be of interest to leadership in the military recruiting services, policymakers who are responsible for military personnel, and to military manpower researchers.

This research was sponsored by OUSD/P&R and conducted within the Forces and Resources Policy Center of the RAND National Defense Research Institute, a federally funded research and development center sponsored by the Office of the Secretary of Defense, the Joint Staff, the Unified Combatant Commands, the Navy, the Marine Corps, the defense agencies, and the defense Intelligence Community. For more information on the RAND Forces and Resources Policy Center, see www.rand.org/nsrd/ndri/centers/frp or contact the director (contact information is provided on the web page).

Contents

Figures and Tables

Figures

Tables

Summary

On January 24, 2013, then–Defense Secretary Leon E. Panetta announced an end to the ban on women in combat. As of January 1, 2016, the armed services must implement efforts to provide equal opportunities regardless of gender. The public nature of the announcement has likely affected potential recruits' views of the military in as yet unknown ways. To provide an early perspective on these effects and how the services and the Office of the Under Secretary of Defense for Personnel and Readiness (OUSD/P&R) can adapt, OUSD/P&R asked RAND to conduct a study exploring these issues. The ultimate goal of the study was to identify approaches for bolstering female recruitment while ground combat jobs are transitioning to include women.

Our Approach

To help inform new approaches for recruiting women, RAND researchers sought to conduct in-depth interviews and focus groups with three key groups of interest. However, insurmountable obstacles prevented us from accessing one important group of interest: civilian youth.

Civilian youth would be an ideal population for exploring why women are not volunteering for military service at the same rates as men, since it is essentially the exact population from which the services draw. Accordingly, civilian youth (and female civilian youth in particular) were our first choice for focus groups. Unfortunately, the period of performance on this project was not long enough to apply for Office of Management and Budget clearance, which takes a minimum of six months and is required when federal funds are used to collect data on members of the public. Instead, with the support of our sponsor, we decided that the recent recruit population would serve as our best available proxy for the civilian youth population, with the full recognition that recent recruits already have a propensity for military service. The recent recruit population would likely still have useful insights into what works and what does not when it comes to recruiting women. These insights alone could help improve recruitment of women, so we proceeded accordingly.

We therefore conducted interviews and focus groups with new recruits (29 enlisted focus groups and four officer groups) and two other key populations of interest: recruiters (15 focus groups) and recruiting leadership (four interviews). Recruit and recruiter participants were solicited from recruiting station locations in Los Angeles, California; Baltimore, Maryland; Richmond, Virginia; and San Antonio, Texas. Recent enlisted recruits who were in the Delayed Entry Program (DEP) were invited to participate at those locations. Officer participants were recent recruits who were waiting to ship out for training.

The focus group discussions and interviews covered the following topics:

- Perceptions and awareness
  - How is the opening of combat roles to women perceived? What are the perceived positives and negatives?

- Influences for joining
  - Were recent events and policy changes (i.e., women in combat, military sexual harassment and sexual assault) a factor in recent recruit decisions to join? (Note that, per the services' request, we did not ask about sexual harassment or assault unless participants raised the issue on their own.)
  - What did recruiters do that was helpful or harmful during the recruiting process? Were there any helpful or harmful things for women in particular?

- Recruiting policies and strategies
  - Are there different approaches to recruiting for men and women? Should there be?
  - What practices are recruiters engaging in to recruit women?
  - What are the obstacles and difficulties associated with recruiting women?
  - What should the military be doing to attract more women?

Discussions with recruits and recruiters were held separately by gender, and the interviewer gender was matched to the gender of the participants, wherever possible. All data collection protocols and procedures received approval from the RAND Human Subjects Protection Committee and through Department of Defense Second Level Review procedures.

Key Findings

Focus groups with recruiters and new recruits yielded a number of interesting insights. Many male recruits in our focus groups reported that their decision to join was not affected by the policy change to open combat jobs to women, and viewed inclusion of women in combat jobs as broadly positive. Others were generally neutral toward the change. For example, multiple male participants expressed the view that women should be allowed into combat if they could meet the same standards as men (e.g., "If they do their job, I can respect it"). Many female participants made positive comments about the change as well (e.g., "they shouldn't be banned").

Recruiters in our focus groups were also not concerned about the impact of this policy change on recruiting, but reported disincentives and barriers to recruiting women. For example, many cited concerns about the possibility of perceived sexual misconduct that can easily occur when male recruiters attempt to recruit female recruits—e.g., "All it takes is one allegation and you are kicked out of recruiting and you are out."

Many women in our focus groups mentioned that female recruiters positively influenced their decision to join the military, and many who did not have a female recruiter suggested that having a female recruiter would have made it easier to join. For instance, one female recruit said, "When you first step into a recruiting office and you see only male recruiters, but you have questions about female problems, you can't really open that conversation up with a man." Some female participants who did not have a female recruiter mentioned that access to female recruiters in other ways helped address that issue. For example, some mentioned that female recruiters had come to their location and hosted discussions to answer their questions, or that a female recruiter in the same recruiting office was made available to talk to them.

Although we did not explicitly ask recruits about sexual harassment and sexual assault in the military (per the services' request), the topic did come up spontaneously in many of our female focus groups, but not in our male focus groups. In the female groups, the topic typically came up in the context of parents' concerns about their daughters joining the military. In cases where it was mentioned, recruits appeared relatively unconcerned about it, and they broadly cited the military's emphasis on protocol and sexual assault prevention training as the reason. However, both recruits and recruiters noted that female recruits' influencers (e.g., parents) were frequently concerned about the issue.

We also asked participants for ideas for how to improve the recruiting processes in general. In response, multiple recruits and recruiters voiced frustration with the amount of time and paperwork that is required as part of the recruiting process. More specifically, participants expressed dissatisfaction with what they viewed as burdensome administrative requirements, which included onerous paperwork, multiple versions of the same form, systems that did not "talk to one another," long wait times due to inefficiencies at Military Entrance Processing Stations, and the requirement to account for recruiters' time in detail. Although these process improvements would likely improve recruiting of men as well as women, some recruiters noted that streamlining these processes is particularly important for recruiting women because female candidates tend to be more likely to change their minds about serving than male candidates. Those recruiters believed that shortening the time and effort required to enlist would give people less time to change their mind and fewer reasons to drop out along the way, which could ultimately help retain more female candidates. Some recruiters also pointed out that reducing administrative burdens on their end would free up more time for them to spend prospecting for new recruits.

When asked for suggestions for ways to recruit more women, many recruits said more access to and greater visibility of female recruiters would help. In addition, both recruiters and recruits also suggested that major changes to advertising were needed. They recommended launching advertising campaigns showing women serving alongside men in a wide range of military jobs, as well as campaigns geared toward debunking the public's misinformed stereotypes of military service. Finally, recruiting leadership reported concern over resources available to them and stated that, although they would very much like to engage in the types of recruiting and outreach that would be ideal for targeting women, they would need more resources to accomplish it.

Recommendations

Based on these findings, we recommend the following focused actions to not only recruit more women but also improve recruiting overall:

- Increase the proportion of female recruiters, strategically place them, and create programs to maximize their impact.
  - Disperse them across recruiting stations to maximize coverage.
  - Ensure that they are highly visible at recruiting events.

  - Create female mentorship programs to make sure all female recruits and potential recruits have access to female recruiters.
  - Organize regular group events (e.g., monthly) so all female recruits have a chance to have face-to-face contact with female recruiters.

- Increase outreach targeted toward women.
  - Create additional advertising and promotional materials highlighting the variety of roles that women fill in the military services and countering stereotypes and misperceptions about military service.
  - Take advantage of recruiting practices that can be focused on women (e.g., women-only events at schools).
  - Conduct follow-up studies to determine the effectiveness of targeted advertising and recruiting events.

- Reduce administrative burdens on recruiters and recruits.
  - Revise requirements on recruiters, such as detailed timekeeping, to reduce the time taken away from recruiting activities.
  - Make better use of technology, such as channeling information from one form to others so that the same information does not have to be entered multiple times.
  - Streamline the recruiting process to shorten the time from initial contact to ship date.

However, as noted in the section above, the cost of such additional recruiting initiatives is an obstacle that was raised by recruiting leadership. Many of the above suggestions—especially those involving the addition of programs, staff, or advertising—would likely require either additional resources or redirection of resources. We therefore discuss the importance of considering costs and other trade-offs further below.

Caveats to Our Recommendations

Although our recommendations follow directly from our focus group findings, we offer a few important caveats that should be considered before any new recruiting policies are implemented.

Limitations of the Study

Do we know these recommendations will lead to measurably better results in recruiting women? The short answer is: no. There are a number of important methodological limitations to our research study, and our recommendations need to be weighed in the context of those limitations.

Most notably, the focus group approach and focus group population both prevent us from being able to say definitively whether our recommendations would have the desired effect. That is, our recommendations are based on opinions, attitudes, and speculation voiced during focus groups and interviews. It is very possible that opinion, attitudes, and speculation may not have validity when it comes to identifying effective strategies for recruiting women. However, in the absence of any other information, we believe it is a starting point for ideas.

In addition, it is important to note again that we were unable to access the ideal population of interest: female civilian youth. Instead, our recommendations come from views expressed by people who have already made the decision to join the military and from military personnel (recruiters and recruiting leadership) who are already steeped in military culture. We therefore fully acknowledge that the participant views that informed our recommendations may be distinctly different from those who chose not to join. Thus, our recommendations might have been different had we interviewed those who chose not to join instead.

However, as noted above, in the absence of any other information, we believe the views of our sample of participants (recent recruits, recruiters, and recruiting leadership) are still useful for generating ideas for improving the recruitment of women. Now that a set of ideas for changes to recruiting practices have been identified, a next step toward a more definitive answers would be to implement some of the recommendations and test out their effectiveness.

Costs, Trade-offs, and Unintended Consequences

As noted above, the recommendations we offered are not cost-free.

Some of the costs come in the form of additional resources, such as separate recruiting materials, special events, and advertising specifically designed to target women. In addition, it is clear from our interviews with recruiters and leadership that more time and effort are needed to recruit women than men, and that women have a higher attrition rate from the DEP. Both are key observations that bear directly on the expected return to additional investments in recruiting women. That is, while the additional resources may increase the number of women recruited, the return on these investments may not be as high (in terms of number of additional bodies recruited and retained) as the return on other recruiting endeavors.

There are also other costs that come in the form of trade-offs or unintended consequences. For example, if more women are placed in recruiting duties, there will be fewer women out performing the mission. This could make women even more of a minority in some situations, which could perpetuate stereotypes and perceptions that there are very few women in certain jobs. And, if women are more likely than men to be sent to recruiting duties or are asked to stay there longer than their male counterparts, it may ultimately hinder their career progression because they will have to spend more time away from their core job. This could hurt women as a whole in the services in the long run, even if it may help with recruiting women. If an effort is made to divert more women to recruiting, then efforts also should be made to prevent negative effects on women's career progression.

In addition (although perhaps this is an obvious point), an increase in the proportion of female new recruits necessarily means a decrease in the proportion of male recruits. It is worth noting that the Office of the Secretary of Defense (OSD) and the services are unlikely to see this as a negative, considering their stated goal to increase representation of women in the services; however, it is a trade-off and therefore is included here as another consideration for policymakers.

These are just a few examples of the many costs, trade-offs, and other potential unintended consequences that need to be considered in decisions about how to proceed. However, these issues, costs, and trade-offs are not insurmountable. Given that OSD and the services have expressed a strong interest in finding ways to recruit more women, the suggestions offered here are still worthy of consideration, assuming that the services are willing to accept the trade-offs discussed above. Nevertheless, closely monitoring the success of such efforts would be wise, to ensure that the obvious trade-offs and costs associated with them are truly justified. In cases where full implementation would be expensive, pilot testing could be an important first step. Such pilot testing would allow for an initial assessment of not only the amount of potential impact of a recommended change, but also an exploration of the potential costs and unintended consequences that might result.

Closing Thoughts

As we usher in a new era of equality for women in the military—one where anyone who can demonstrate the abilities necessary to do the job can serve in that job—the number of jobs available to women will increase dramatically. As a result, women in uniform will likely begin to be increasingly visible in jobs across the services (especially in the Army and Marine Corps, where the majority of the jobs were previously closed). These increased opportunities offer new avenues for women to have a successful military career and could be an important driver for generating interest among women who may not have previously considered serving. This policy change therefore brings with it new chances to grow the representation of women in the service.

This study was designed to provide initial suggestions for how the services could take steps to generate such new interest. Overall, our results suggest that more certainly could be done to target women who have not previously expressed interest; however, as noted above, such efforts come with added costs that need to be considered. Nevertheless, we offer a number of initial suggestions for actions that could be pursued to help recruit more female youth. How successful will these efforts be increasing representation of women in the services? That question can best be answered by implementing the suggestions discussed here and following up with additional research on their effectiveness. As such, this work is just a first step toward finding the policies that are most effective at increasing representation of women in the services. More work will undoubtedly be needed.

Acknowledgments

We are deeply appreciative of Dennis Drogo and Evelyn Dyer, Office of the Under Secretary of Defense for Personnel and Readiness/Readiness and Force Management/Military Personnel Policy/Accession Policy, for their overall support and guidance throughout this project. Stephanie Miller, director of Accession Policy, and Chris Arendt, Accession Policy, provided additional insight and guidance. Katherine Helland and Taylor Fairley of Department of Defense Joint Advertising Marketing Research and Studies provided data and insight into their research findings and suggested additional research questions. At RAND, we acknowledge Lindsay Daugherty, Irina Danescu, and David Schulker for assisting with the focus groups. Julie Ann Tajiri and Donna White provided invaluable administrative support. We would also like to thank peer reviewers Ryan Brown, Coreen Farris, and Jennifer Lamping-Lewis for their thoughtful and constructive comments.

This study would not have been possible without the cooperation of the many servicemembers who graciously agreed to speak with us. Multiple recruiting commanders and recruiting station commanders across all four services helped coordinate our site visits, focus groups, and interviews. Most of all, we thank the recent recruits, recruiters, and senior leaders who agreed to share their thoughts with us.

Abbreviations

DEP	Delayed Entry Program
DoD	U.S. Department of Defense
HRC	Human Resources Command
JAMRS	Joint Advertising Market Research and Studies
MEPS	Military Entrance Processing Station
MOS	military occupational specialty
OMB	Office of Management and Budget
OSD	Office of the Secretary of Defense
OUSD/P&R	Office of the Under Secretary of Defense for Personnel and Readiness
STEM	science, technology, engineering, and math

CHAPTER ONE

Introduction

Beginning with the Women's Armed Services Integration Act of 1948, women have become increasingly integrated into the U.S. military. Before 1967, the proportion of women allowed in the military was limited to 2 percent in the enlisted force and 10 percent in the officer corps, and women were barred from admittance to the service academies until 1974. Since the end of conscription in 1973, however, the number of opportunities available to women in the military has grown. As a result, from 1973 to 2010 the proportion of women increased significantly, growing from 2 percent to 14 percent among enlistees and 4 percent to 16 percent among commissioned officers (Patten and Parker, 2011). However, women were still barred from assignment to units whose "primary mission is to engage in direct combat on the ground" by a 1994 Secretary of Defense Memorandum on the direct ground combat definition and assignment rule (Aspin, 1994). Under this policy, women were not permitted to serve in ground combat career fields, such as infantry, armor, combat engineers, and special operations, which meant that significant numbers of occupations in the Army and Marine Corps were still off-limits to women. On January 24, 2013, then–Defense Secretary Leon E. Panetta announced an end to the ban on women in direct ground combat roles, essentially removing all remaining barriers to female service in the military. The services were directed to develop implementation plans for phasing women into these new roles by May 15, 2013, with full integration of women into the services to be completed no later than January 1, 2016 (Panetta, 2013).

In preparation for the implementation of these changes, the Office of the Under Secretary of Defense for Personnel and Readiness (OUSD/P&R) asked RAND to help explore how the opening of combat jobs to women might affect recruiting and identify ways to mitigate any potential negative impacts. OUSD/P&R also asked for suggestions for ways to increase the recruitment of women in general, as women are still significantly underrepresented in the force as a whole.

In response to OUSD/P&R's request, we outlined three main research questions as the focus of our study:

- What are potential recruits' attitudes towards the policy change?
- What are the main influences for decisions to (or not to) join, and how might that differ for women relative to men?
- What are the services' current recruiting strategies and policies for recruiting women?

We conducted focus groups and interviews to help address these questions, and, based on our findings, we present recommendations for changes to recruiting practices that could be useful in helping to attract and recruit candidates after the change is implemented, with particular emphasis on suggestions for recruiting more women.

Background on Women in Combat and Other Relevant Issues of Interest

There were three topic areas that we attempted to address in our data collection effort. The major impetus for this study was to examine the recruiting impact of the policy change to open combat jobs to women. However, OUSD/P&R also expressed interest in the potential recruiting impact of sexual harassment and sexual assault in the military (given high-profile events) and trends relating to propensity to join the military. Below, we provide further background on these issues of interest and briefly discuss how we addressed them in our data collection effort.

Integration of Women Into Combat Roles

In 2013, Panetta rescinded the 1994 Direct Ground Combat Exclusion policy that had prevented women from serving in ground combat jobs in the military. He gave the services until the end of 2015 to establish valid gender-neutral standards for those occupations or to provide a compelling reason that the jobs should remain closed to women. The services complied, and on December 3, 2015, then–Defense Secretary Ash Carter announced that, as of January 2016, all military occupations and positions would be opened to women.

Among the services, this change is likely to have a bigger impact on the Marine Corps and the Army, as a larger share of their job specialties were previously identified as ground combat roles under the 1994 definition. The Navy has allowed women to serve on surface ships since 1978 and authorized women to serve on submarines in April 2010. One of the Navy's main constraints in opening positions to women is the conversion of existing platforms to accommodate female berthing spaces. Approximately 15 percent (5,600 or so) of the positions that the Navy will open to women are within or connected with the special operations community (Defense Advisory Committee on Women in the Services, 2014). Prior to the 2013 decision, the Air Force already had over 99 percent of its positions open to women. In response to the policy change, the Air Force will be opening less than 5,000 special operations and combat rescue positions to women.

Because the major impetus for the study was the change to the combat exclusion policy, our study was designed to focus most heavily on the impact of this policy change on recruiting. For that reason, some of our focus group questions were designed to explicitly ask about the combat exclusion policy change. In addition, although the primary focus was on the impacts to recruiting of women, we were interested in how it would affect recruitment of men as well. We therefore held focus groups with men and women separately. Our focus groups took place in fall 2015, before ground combat jobs were officially opened to women but after the combat exclusion policy had been lifted.

Sexual Harassment and Sexual Assault in the Military

Political and media interest in sexual harassment and assault in the military has skyrocketed. At the same time, there has also been increased media coverage of sexual assault and gender issues in the civilian world, such as on college campuses. This is in part due to societal evolution in thinking on sexual assault and harassment. Today, such behavior (both in the public and the military) is much less tolerated than in decades past. Therefore, when related high-profile events in the military have surfaced, the issues have made headlines. Recent scandals in the military that have drawn such attention include the removal of male Air Force basic training instructors at Lackland Air Force Base following charges of sexual misconduct. In addition, several senior leaders, including individuals in charge of military programs designed to address sexual assault issues, have faced allegations of sexual assault.

The media have not only responded to the high-profile scandals, but they have also continued to feature human interest stories and reviews of reports on scientific research related to sexual assault and harassment in the military. For example, in 2007, the *New York Times Magazine* published an article that tied female servicemembers' psychological trauma with combat-related activities as well as sexual harassment and assault experienced during deployments (Corbett, 2007). In 2012, the Sundance Film Festival screened *The Invisible War,* an investigative documentary that profiled male and female veterans and their physical, legal, and psychological challenges in coping with the aftermath of sexual assault while serving in the military.

Researchers have also tackled these issues in the military with large-scale studies. For example, according to a congressionally mandated study surveying 170,000 servicemembers in 2014, nearly 5 percent of active-duty women and 1 percent of active-duty men reported experiencing one or more sexual assaults in the past year, and 26 percent of active-duty women and 7 percent of active-duty men reported experiencing sexual harassment or gender discrimination in the past year (Morral et al., 2014). In addition, a 2012 workplace and gender relations survey of active-duty servicemembers found that 30 percent of women and 6 percent of men experienced unwanted sexual contact prior to entering the military, a number that appears to be higher than what has been estimated in some studies of civilians (Defense Manpower Data Center, 2013).[1]

Given the growth in media attention that sexual harassment and assault in the military has received, it is no surprise that the Office of the Secretary of Defense (OSD) is concerned that it may impact recruiting. As a result, OSD asked us to explore whether sexual harassment and assault appears to be a factor in recruiting more women. However, as we discuss further in the next chapter, the services asked that we not raise this issue directly in our focus groups, out of concern that it might create concerns in previously unworried candidates. We therefore did not include questions that directly asked about sexual harassment or assault and explored this topic only when it naturally came up in discussion. We base our findings about the role of sexual harassment/assault concerns in ability to recruit women on how often the topic came up without prompting during discussions.

Propensity for Military Service

Women in general have a lower propensity to enlist than men. Recent trends in propensity for military service may raise questions about the impact of certain issues (women in combat, military sexual harassment and sexual assault) on recruiting efforts. Approximately 26 percent of all youth who indicate that they will join the military actually enlist, although additional youth may have attempted to join but did not qualify (Ford et al., 2014). Previous studies have found that propensity to enlist and likelihood of joining are influenced by a number of factors, including norms of service in a geographic area. Potential recruits in the South and the Midwest are about one-third more likely to enlist than those in the Northeast, and each percentage point increase in the percentage of veterans in one's zip code is associated with being over 600 times more likely to join the military (Ford et al., 2014). In addition, each percentage

[1] While there is not a comparable gender relations survey for the civilian workforce and student populations, the National College Women Study, for instance, surveyed college women in 2005, finding that 11.5 percent had "experienced a forcible or incapacitated rape in their lifetime" (Kilpatrick et al., 2007).

point increase in the enlistment rate by zip code was also associated with being 380 times more likely to join the military (Ford et al., 2014). A study of military propensity of young women suggested that women who join typically have a clear set of education goals and career aspirations and are familiar with the military, either through participation in Junior Reserve Officers' Training Corps or by growing up in a family with strong military traditions (Berkowitz, Achatz, and Westat, 1999).

Study Approach

We conducted focus groups and interviews with recent military recruits, recruiters, and recruiting leadership to address the above research questions. We chose focus groups as our mode of data collection because of their ability to surface nuanced insights, concerns, and varied experiences and to allow opportunities to probe for greater detail on any relevant topics. The resulting rich, nuanced information can provide unique insights for informing policy decisions about improving the recruiting process. We also intentionally designed our research questions to be broad, open-ended, and general in nature to allow respondents to generate their own ideas without being biased or led in a particular direction. This design was particularly important in determining whether respondents would raise certain hot-button issues, such as sexual harassment and assault, without prompting. The focus group methodology and findings are the main focus of the remainder of this report.

Organization of This Report

Chapter Two describes the methodology used in our interviews and focus groups with recent recruits, recruiters, and recruiting leadership. Chapters Three, Four, and Five map directly onto the three research questions listed at the beginning of this chapter. Chapter Three discusses recent military recruits' perceptions about women in the military and the possibility of women serving in combat. Chapter Four covers factors that are important in recruits' decisions to join the military. Chapter Five examines recruiting policies and strategies, including current practices and guidance. Finally, Chapter Six describes recommended courses of action to improve recruitment of both men and women into the military, based on the main findings from our discussions with recent recruits, recruiters, and recruiter leadership.

The focus group discussion protocols are provided in Appendix A. Appendix B contains the entire set of themes we identified in the focus groups and interviews, including additional responses other than those discussed in the main body of the report.

CHAPTER TWO

Focus Group Methodology

We conducted in-depth interviews and focus groups with new recruits, recruiters, and recruiting leadership across the United States to gain firsthand perspectives on the recruiting impact of efforts to provide equal opportunities regardless of gender.[1] The focus groups were designed to allow for comparisons across genders as well as services.

Overarching Purpose, Design, and Protocol of Focus Groups

Our focus groups were designed to expand on the three overarching research questions stated in Chapter One. However, in creating a more-specific list of questions for our focus groups, we took care that our questions did not directly overlap with any already-existing information germane to the topics. To do this, we reviewed a variety of U.S. Department of Defense (DoD) Joint Advertising Market Research and Studies (JAMRS) research products summarizing analyses of surveys and focus group data sources. Topics covered by existing JAMRS surveys and focus groups included awareness and opinion information (such as what people in the general population people think about the military and what media sources they use to learn about news and the military) and opinions of those who were either not in the military (i.e., youth poll) or were uncertain about joining the military (JAMRS focus groups of "fence sitters"). We also met with JAMRS representatives to discuss areas where our focus groups could provide value-added or supplemental information and developed our focus group questions with their guidance and input.

The following topics were among those identified as being both useful and complementary to the existing JAMRS information:

- Perceptions and awareness
  - How is the opening of combat roles to women perceived? What are the perceived positives and negatives?

- Influences for joining
  - Were recent events and policy changes (i.e., women in combat, military sexual harassment and sexual assault) a factor in recent recruit decisions to join?
  - What did recruiters do that was helpful or harmful during the recruiting process? Were there any helpful or harmful things for women in particular?

[1] All data collection protocols and procedures received approval from the RAND Human Subjects Protection Committee and through DoD Second Level Review procedures.

- Recruiting policies and strategies
  - Are there different approaches to recruiting for men and women? Should there be?
  - What practices are recruiters engaging in to recruit women?
  - What are the obstacles and difficulties associated with recruiting women?
  - What should the military be doing to attract more women?

We also consulted with JAMRS and our project sponsor in identifying the populations of interest for the discussions. Based on the broad topics and the specific questions above that were identified, we decided to focus our efforts on recent recruits, recruiters, and recruiting leadership as our target populations.

We would, however, like to note that that civilian youth (not recent recruits) would be a more ideal population for gaining insights into many of these issues, and especially for exploring why women are not interested in military service. Accordingly, civilian youth (and female civilian youth in particular) was our first choice population for the focus groups. But, unfortunately, the period of performance on this project was not long enough to allow for us to apply for Office of Management and Budget (OMB) clearance (an approval process that takes a minimum of six months), which is required when federal funds are used to collect data on members of the public. Instead, with the support of our sponsor, we decided that the recent recruit population would have to serve as our best available proxy for the civilian youth population, with the full recognition that recent recruits already have a propensity for military service since they joined the service.

We therefore fully acknowledge that recent recruits are distinctly different from those who chose not to join and that their views may not represent those of greatest interest for this work: namely, women who are not interested in military service. Nevertheless, the recent recruit population would likely still have useful insights into what works and what does not work when it comes to recruiting women. That insight alone could help improve recruitment of women, so we proceeded accordingly.

Sampling of Focus Group Locations

We conducted focus groups with active-duty enlisted personnel and officers in the Army, Navy, Air Force, and Marine Corps Delayed Entry Program (DEP) pools from July 2015 to November 2015. Ideally, we would have conducted focus groups with civilians who were considering joining the military. However, conducting interviews with members of the public would require OMB review and approval, a lengthy process. We therefore looked for military members who were most similar to people who are considering joining the military. While recruits in the DEP remain in their original locations to await basic training, they are considered military members. These recruits were therefore accessible and could be recruited for the focus groups. Having already decided to enter the military, these recruits constituted a different population than potential recruits. Yet because these recruits had only recently joined the military and had not yet entered basic training, their attitudes and information about the military should be most similar—among military members—to those of potential recruits.

We were particularly interested in whether men and women would share views or have different views on a number of issues. We were also concerned that men and women might be less than forthright in some of their responses if the other gender was present. For that reason, we opted to hold separate focus groups for women and men. We were also able to match the gender of the interviewer to the gender of the group in nearly all of the focus groups. Recruiter focus groups were also conducted separately by gender.

Focus groups for enlisted recruits in the DEP were held in Los Angeles, California; Baltimore, Maryland; Richmond, Virginia; and San Antonio, Texas, along with phone interviews when in-person focus groups could not be scheduled. Recruiter and officer focus groups were conducted in the same locations. However, due to scheduling constraints, many of the recruiter interviews/focus groups were conducted via phone. We selected the focus groups using the following criteria, chosen in conjunction with our OUSD/P&R sponsor:

- all services available at each location
- similar numbers of available male and female participants at each location
- sufficient geographic diversity between locations, so that participants' opinions should not overly represent a particular locale or region.[2]

The intent behind these criteria was to identify focus group locations that would broadly reflect opinions across the military. We selected locations that, as much as possible, would satisfy these criteria. In each location, we requested that each service nominate participants for two male and two female groups, with six to ten participants per group. In practice, the number of individuals in each focus group depended on the number of willing and available individuals in the DEP at each location. Often we succeeded in conducting focus groups with six to ten men, but it was harder to locate six to ten women in each location. Therefore, the number of individuals in the focus groups ranged from one to ten, depending on availability in each location. Although we did not record the exact number of individuals in each group, nearly all of the focus groups had three or more participants, and the majority of the focus groups had five to ten participants. Table 2.1 shows the final number of enlisted recruit focus groups, broken out by gender, military service, and location. Tables 2.2 and 2.3 show the final number of officer recruit and recruiter groups, respectively.

Due to time and scheduling constraints, we were limited to four focus groups with recent officer recruits. We conducted two male focus groups with Marines, one female focus group with Marines, and one interview with a female Air Force officer. The opinions these officers expressed, therefore, reflect the perspectives of both genders, but not always both genders across services.

New Recruit Focus Group Procedures

We conducted focus groups with new military recruits to understand potential recruits' attitudes toward the military and the policy change and the influences on their decisions to join the military. Focus groups were typically conducted in recruiting stations and sometimes in physical training locations (e.g., gymnasiums). Although the majority of the focus groups were conducted in-person, two focus groups in the Richmond location were held via conference calls due to a scheduling conflict that arose after the researchers were on-site. In addition to

[2] Regional differences in propensity for service (e.g., respondents in the South and Midwest are about one-third more likely to enlist than those in the Northeast [Ford et al., 2014]) suggest that there may also be regional differences in attitudes.

Table 2.1
Number of New Enlisted Recruit Focus Groups by Service and Location

	By Service				By Location				Total
Focus Group	Army	Navy	Air Force	Marine Corps	Baltimore	Richmond	Los Angeles	San Antonio	
Female	2	4	4	4	3	2	4	5	14
Male	3	4	4	4	3	3	4	5	15
Total	5	8	8	8	6	5	8	10	29

Table 2.2
Number of Officer Interview/Focus Groups by Service and Location

	By Service				By Location				Total
Focus Group	Army	Navy	Air Force	Marine Corps	Baltimore	Richmond	Los Angeles	San Antonio	
Female	0	0	1	1	1	0	0	1	2
Male	0	0	0	2	1	0	0	1	2
Total	0	0	1	3	2	0	0	2	4

Table 2.3
Number of Recruiter Interview/Focus Groups by Service and Location

	By Service				By Location				Total
Focus Group	Army	Navy	Air Force	Marine Corps	Baltimore	Richmond	Los Angeles	San Antonio	
Female	1	2	3	2	2	1	3	2	8
Male	1	2	3	1	1	2	2	2	7
Total	2	4	6	3	3	3	5	4	15

obtaining voluntary consent, we also asked participants for their permission to record audio to supplement our notes during the discussion. Participants were also informed that the information they provided would be treated as confidential, to be reported only as group data with no identifying information.

To open discussion, we asked participants to each briefly state their background (where they were from, etc.). Next we asked questions from a predetermined research protocol (see Appendix A), probing on specific points or from specific individuals to obtain more detailed information. Questions were designed to address our main research questions, in particular, to assess

1. awareness of the new DoD policy regarding the opening of formerly closed occupations to women among recruiters and service applicants
2. whether and how the recruiting environment may have changed as the result of this decision
3. how recruiters may have changed their recruiting behaviors to accommodate the new policy and attract more qualified women
4. how applicants' views of military service may have changed as a result of the new policy creating more opportunities for women in today's military.

We deliberately did not ask specific questions about sexual harassment and sexual assault, even though this was a key issue for OUSD/P&R. This was due to concern from the services that raising the topic of sexual harassment and sexual assault in the military could have unintended negative effects on the recruits' desire to join the military. Because of this concern, we did not include explicit questions about sexual harassment and sexual assault. Instead, we asked open-ended questions on what concerns recruits or their influencers had about joining the military; whether the role of women in the military or in combat played a role in the decision to join the military; concerns about serving in a majority-male organization (female recruit groups only); and whether female recruits had sought perspectives from other women about joining the military. We then observed whether participants would raise, unprompted, the topic of sexual harassment and sexual assault. Unsurprisingly, multiple participants across focus groups raised this topic. These results are reported in later sections of this report.

The focus groups lasted approximately 60 minutes. One RAND researcher served as facilitator, with another researcher serving as notetaker. In most cases, we matched gender of the researchers (facilitator and notetaker) with that of the focus group in an effort to ensure that participants felt they could speak openly and freely about gender differences, opinions, and issues in the military.

Recruiter Interviews and Focus Groups

We conducted focus groups and interviews with recruiters to obtain information about recruiting policies and strategies. We also wanted a complementary perspective on potential recruits' attitudes toward the military and the policy change and on influences on recruits' decisions to join the military. The number of recruiters in each focus group depended on the availability and willingness of the recruiters. As a result, some recruiters were interviewed in groups, while others were interviewed individually. The topics covered included a recruiter's experience and training prior to recruiting; methods for identifying new recruits; incentives both for the recruiters and the recruits; differences in recruiting men and women; the role of influencers; and responses to the policy change allowing women in combat roles (see Appendix A for the full protocol). For recruiters, there were no concerns that questions about sexual harassment and sexual assault in the military would have a negative impact on recruiting. We could therefore ask explicitly about recruiters' experiences as to whether female recruits were concerned about sexual harassment or sexual assault, and how they as recruiters addressed those concerns. As with new recruits, the recruiter participants were informed that their responses would be confidential. Interviews lasted approximately 60 minutes.

Leadership Interviews

For insight about current recruiting policies and practices, we interviewed by phone the commander of each of the four recruiting services. In each of these interviews, other members of the commander's staff were present and provided additional input. The topics covered included whether and how each recruiting service recruited women; recruiting best practices; recruiting policy changes in response to recent issues (e.g., opening of combat jobs to women; military sexual harassment and sexual assault); and recommended improvements to recruiting (see Appendix A for the full protocol). As with the recruiters, we could deliberately ask about these policies as well as initiatives intended to address the issue of sexual harassment without being concerned about any potential impact on recruiting. Interviews lasted approximately 45 minutes. All commanders agreed to be acknowledged as participants in this study and to be cited as a source of information. Note that because the leadership interviews focused entirely on recruiting practices and policies, the results of those interviews are discussed in Chapter Five.

Recruitment

We worked with OUSD/P&R to identify appropriate individuals to participate in the interviews and focus groups. Our sponsor provided points of contact at each of the services to help identify these individuals. We supplied OUSD/P&R and theservices with invitation letters describing the purpose of the study, and inviting them to participate in either interviews or focus groups. Each service then contacted the individuals they had identified. On behalf of OUSD/P&R and RAND, each service's local point of contact emailed or called recruits to participate in a voluntary focus group on a specific date. When possible, these dates were scheduled around preexisting DEP events (e.g., physical fitness training and testing) for convenience and to maximize the potential number of participants.

To reduce the burden and cost on respondents, we coordinated these focus group efforts with a concurrent OUSD/P&R-sponsored project that also called for focus groups with new recruits. This was intended to reduce the time required for the services to schedule site visits, and to streamline the onsite focus group process so that respondents would need to spend less time on procedural matters related to the focus groups. In addition, we conducted interviews by phone to reduce the need for respondents (i.e., recruiters, recruiting leadership) to attend an in-person meeting.

Analysis

We systematically coded the responses from the focus groups and interviews with the goal of (1) identifying the most common themes and (2) providing a comprehensive picture of the range of comments raised during our discussion, regardless of their frequency. First, we built a draft coding framework that included the three broad groupings corresponding to the original research questions: perceptions and awareness, influences for joining, and recruiting policies and strategies. Starting from these broad groupings, two coders (the first and second authors) individually reviewed a subset of the data (five focus groups) and jointly identified commonly mentioned responses for each research question (actual number identified ranged from two to 12). The purpose of this exercise was to be able to group similar kinds of information together into categories. Responses could apply to multiple subtopics, and in those instances, were coded in multiple categories. Additionally, illustrative quotes were marked for easy extraction.

As an example of this coding, in one question, recent recruits were asked about what had appealed to them about joining the military. Responses from the data subset included pay, education benefits, travel, pride, and others. We created coding categories for each of these topics, including an "other" category to capture topics besides those we had explicitly identified. We also used an overall "other" section to capture any other conversation that was not an explicit response to a question in the protocol and did not fit into any of the broad groupings of topics.

Each coder then individually coded two more sets of focus groups to test the coding scheme. The coders then reconvened to ensure that their coding aligned. Based on the results of this discussion, the coders jointly revised the coding scheme to consolidate overlapping and redundant topics. For example, an initial theme corresponding to an interview question ("suggested changes that would have made the decision to join easier") was removed because it overlapped with a similar question ("recommended changes to improve recruiting").

Once the researchers finalized the coding scheme, all remaining focus groups were coded. To ensure reliability, the coders then compared the two individually completed data sets and reconciled substantial differences. This reconciliation process involved identifying questions in which the two coders differed by more than three or four focus groups (which we considered to be a "substantial" difference), and then discussing and recoding responses for individual focus groups until they fit within the range of 12.5 percentiles (i.e., eight equal groups that added up to 100 percent). If, for instance, according to one coder, 9 percent of focus groups mentioned a particular theme, and according to the other coder, 11 percent of the groups mentioned that same theme, we did not reconcile any further because the percentages fell within the 0-percent to 12.5-percent percentile. We then reported the more conservative coding estimate (in this example, mentions in 9 percent of focus groups). The vast majority of differences or discrepancies in coding were due to keystroke errors or the way each coder interpreted the coding scheme. For example, coder A may have thought that concerns about "injury/death" included psychological injury (e.g., posttraumatic stress disorder), and coder B did not. In the reconciliation process, the coders decided that concerns about injury/death should include posttraumatic stress disorder, and coder B changed responses accordingly. We then analyzed the resulting data to identify salient and overarching themes, recurring concepts and language, and patterns of beliefs among the recent recruits.

Analysis of recruiter focus group data followed the same procedures as those for the recent recruit focus groups. The two coders created an initial coding scheme, individually coded a subset, and then iteratively refined the coding scheme. Because the two coders had jointly coded and discussed coding for both the recent recruits and recruiters, this was assumed to be sufficient training for reliable coding. One coder therefore created the finalized coding scheme and implemented it, without postcoding reconciliation.

To present the resulting themes, we report the percentage of focus groups in which at least one respondent in that group mentioned each theme. Participants within a group often expressed differing opinions on topics. As such, these percentages reflect the breadth of responses across focus groups by illustrating how often opposing viewpoints were raised. By coding the differing opinions separately and then reporting the frequency of groups in which they were mentioned, we were able to capture the full range of responses.

Because we conducted relatively few (four) leadership interviews, we did not explicitly code them for themes. Rather, each coder individually extracted themes and quotes, which we combined in the final results. Given the small number of officer focus groups, we also extracted themes and quotes without using an explicit coding scheme.

Interpreting the Coding Results

As explained above, we calculated the percentages of focus groups where at least one person mentioned a point or issue. Those percentages are presented in the next three chapters and in Appendix B. However, when interpreting the percentages, a few things should be kept in mind.

First, we offer readers the following broad statements regarding the purpose and limitations of the focus group analyses reported here:

- The point of the coding analyses is not to state precisely how many participants or what percentage of groups held a particular viewpoint. The findings are illustrative and descriptive, intended to convey the overall relative magnitude of an observation across groups. In other words, some viewpoints were mentioned in many groups, whereas other viewpoints were mentioned in very few.
- Because there were a small number of focus groups, results stated in proportions are subject to wide variability. For example, a difference of just one focus group reporting a particular viewpoint can amount to what might appear to be large differences in the proportions (e.g., seven out of the 14 female focus groups = 50 percent, whereas six out of the 14 = 43 percent), even when those differences are neither statistically significant nor practically meaningful. As a result, differences in proportions reported should not be interpreted as conveying statistical significance.
- Although we did intentionally sample participants from recruiting stations on the coasts and in the middle of the United States to help ensure a range of perspectives, the results could have been different had we included different recruiting stations or even different participants from within those recruiting stations. Results are not generalizable beyond the groups we included in our study.

Second, we advise caution in reviewing the percentages themselves. For one thing, it is important to note that the percentages represent the number of *focus groups* in which at least one participant mentioned the comment. The percentage cannot be interpreted as the percentage of *recruits* that agree with that statement. For example, we found that in 79 and 80 percent of the female and male focus groups, respectively, someone expressed a desire to go into combat. This does not mean that 79 percent of the female participants were willing, nor does it mean that 80 percent of the male participants were willing. This also cannot be interpreted to mean that the percentage of women who would be willing to go into combat is the same as the percentage of men willing. Instead, it merely means that there is sufficient interest by *some* women that it should not be disregarded.

Readers are also cautioned that because these are counts of spontaneous comments, the statistics cannot be interpreted to imply the converse of a statement. For example, while 13 percent of male focus groups had someone who explicitly stated that they would go into combat if called upon, it does not mean that participants in the remaining 87 percent of focus groups would not be willing to do so if called upon.

In addition, we note that some comments are not mutually exclusive. For example, when asked about the benefits to joining the military, a single individual often listed multiple benefits. The focus group percentages we report for each reason do not necessarily reflect opinions voiced by different people. So, when we say that education benefits were mentioned in 93 percent of focus groups and opportunity to travel in 71 percent, it is entirely possible that the same people who mentioned travel also mentioned education.

On the other hand, when comments are mutually exclusive, they do reflect views from different individuals. Instances where we present percentages for opposing views are such cases. For example, approximately 75 percent of female recruiter focus groups mentioned using the same approach for recruiting men as recruiting women, whereas approximately 65 percent of female recruiter focus groups mentioned using different approaches. These are opposing views on how they approach recruiting of women, and they reflect real differences across individuals.

Lastly, we note that the coding results need to be interpreted carefully, taking into consideration the limitations to inferences that can be made using results from a focus group methodology. In this study, our focus group discussions were guided conversations, and responses were entirely open-ended; we posed questions to the group and participants generated responses relating to whatever topics came to mind and in whatever order seemed appropriate for the conversation. As a result, the information we obtained is different from what would be obtained in other ways.

For example, survey participants are often asked to choose a response for every question (e.g., "Check off all of the statements you agree with" or "Rate how strongly you agree with the following statement"). In such closed-ended surveys, counts of participants or even counts of groups agreeing with a viewpoint can be used to definitively determine how much agreement exists in a given population. However, in the case of open-ended response formats, such as focus groups, the conditions may not always allow for participants to voice a viewpoint they nonetheless hold. It is possible that a topic of conversation can change before participants have fully thought about or answered a question. It is also possible for a question to be phrased slightly differently from group to group, prompting a different type of response. In some cases, participants may simply not think to articulate a particular view, even if they wholeheartedly agree with it.

As a result, it is very possible that in focus groups a viewpoint may not be voiced by anyone in the group, even if it is a viewpoint held by some or all of the participants. In our study, this means that the percentages we report may underrepresent the number of groups in which a particular viewpoint was held. To further clarify which views tended to be widely held (despite not being mentioned in every group), we also offer a variety of qualitative observations from the discussions (this is discussed further in the next section).

To reiterate this last point succinctly, focus groups are not good at determining *how many* people in a population hold a particular viewpoint. That is best estimated through a closed-ended survey of a representative sample. We have not sought to determine, for example, how many recent recruits support the opening up of combat jobs to women. Instead, the focus groups are useful for showing the range of viewpoints held by our participants, and for noting which topics, issues, and viewpoints came up in many groups (as opposed to very few groups). Any inferences beyond these, however, are not appropriate.

Putting the Focus Group Results in Context

In addition to presenting percentages of focus groups reporting each type of comment, we further explore the issues and points that were raised by our participants in two ways. First, we explain the issue or topic further and, when it would be useful, provide some illustrative quotations from our participants and/or paraphrase some of their comments. Second, we supplement many of the percentages with summative qualitative impressions of the discussions.

We formed these qualitative impressions over the course of our observations of the focus group discussions. As a reminder, the focus groups were structured as a conversation, not as a poll, so we do not have exact numbers of participants agreeing with each comment. That is, we asked a question, probed for more information, and then asked for more thoughts from others in the group. While some extended discussion on a topic took place, we waited to see whether others spoke up with similar or different views. When people did not speak up with differing views, we asked whether anyone disagreed or had a different thought and probed for more information if someone said yes. In other words, because of the conversational nature of focus groups, it simply is not possible to collect exact numbers of participants who agreed or disagreed with each statement.

Nevertheless, having attended the focus groups, we do in many cases have a clear sense for general agreement or disagreement with a particular sentiment. Sometimes one person would speak up and we would see others nodding. Sometimes one person would speak and others would provide additional supporting examples, stories, or comments to show their agreement. Sometimes multiple people would voice their disagreement with something someone else said. On a few occasions, we did ask for a show of hands to confirm our general impression of the level of agreement among the participants; however, doing so can disrupt the flow of the conversation, so we did so only when it felt appropriate and helpful. Even in those instances, we did not record an exact head count. Instead, we formed a general impression about the level of agreement within the groups (i.e., many agreed, very few agreed). Thus, at the end of the focus groups, we had a general sense for the level of agreement at the individual level on many of the topics, even though we did not have exact counts.

Those general impressions that we formed from the discussion are extremely rich additional information that goes beyond just the numbers distilled from the coding process. They reveal less-quantifiable but still valid insights that can come from focus group discussions. Instances where we make statements like "Many of our recruiters felt that . . ." or "Some of our participants disagreed . . ." are examples of those summative impressions of the individual level of agreement within the focus groups.

CHAPTER THREE

Perceptions About and Attitudes Towards Women in the Military and in Combat

As the military moves to fully integrate women into combat, willingness to serve may be affected in as yet unknown ways. In our discussions with recruits, we therefore sought to explore perceptions and attitudes related to women serving in the military in general and specifically in combat. In this chapter, we describe several key perceptions and attitudes mentioned in those discussions. We start with an overview of attitudes towards women in the military and in combat. Following that, we discuss perceived concerns about and benefits of having women serving in combat. Lastly, we describe participants' perceptions of the importance of eliminating misconceptions to attract more women to military service. Figure 3.1 provides highlights of the comments from recruits.

Recruiters were not directly asked about potential recruits' attitudes towards women in the military or their attitudes towards the change in the policy regarding women in combat, and they did not tend to volunteer comments about either topic during the discussion. However, we did ask recruiters about women's interest in serving in combat roles, and we include their views on this issue in that section, along with the views from the recent recruits. Recruiter insights are discussed only in those sections where applicable.

Attitudes Towards Women in the Military

Many recruits had a broadly positive view of women in the military. In some groups, when asked, people responded neutrally. However, as shown in Figure 3.1, positive perceptions of women in the military were mentioned in a large percentage of both male and female enlisted focus groups. In groups in which no positive statements were made, participants tended to be simply neutral towards the issue, saying essentially "it doesn't matter."

For example, among the female enlisted groups, some cited the importance of equal opportunity: e.g., "I see it as an equal thing; it shouldn't be a problem if it's a boy or girl. It's great that women can join up." Others mentioned wanting to disprove gender stereotypes (e.g., "People think you have to be more masculine, that isn't true") and break down gender barriers ("[There are] so many misconceptions about women in the military, [I] want to dismantle those," "I love to challenge the gender norms . . . we will prove those things wrong"). Some female officer participants were similarly enthusiastic. According to one female officer,

> I think it's great because it strengthens the military. Women are capable to do a lot of the jobs. Even if most women can't meet the standards but there is one woman who can do it she deserves to be able to do it.

Figure 3.1
Enlisted Recruit Focus Group Responses: Views on Women in the Military and in Combat

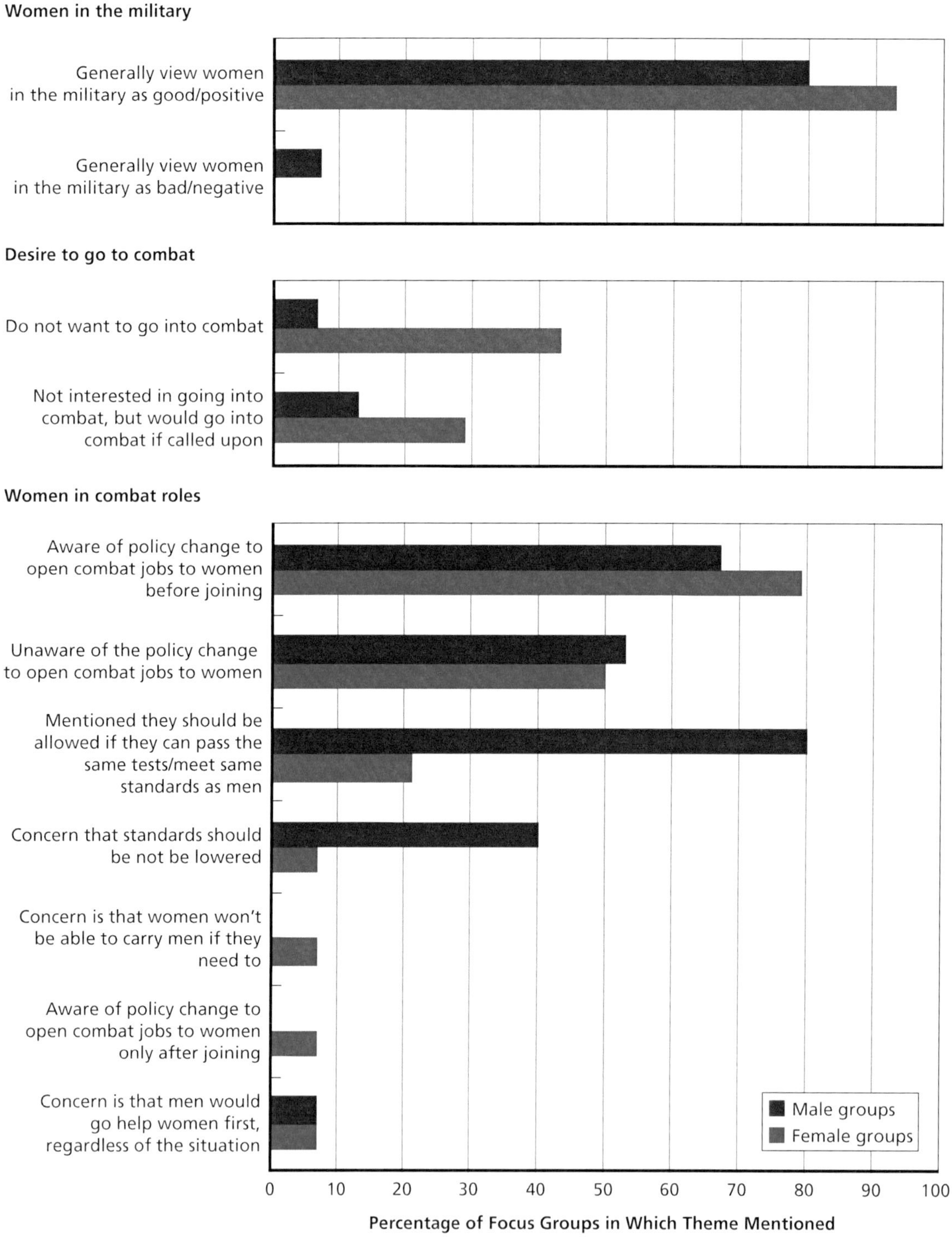

RAND *RR1538-3.1*

Among the male enlisted groups, positive comments included general affirmation ("It's good, I have no issues with it"), as well as references to fairness ("If someone can do the job, they should get to do the job") and a better social environment ("I think it's essential to have a well-rounded atmosphere . . . it feels more normal"). Some male officers who had expressed concerns about women in the military balanced these concerns against the potential benefits for the military, such as increased diversity, and referred to successful deployments of female special operators and all-female counterinsurgency liaisons. One officer indicated that "Women in the Marine Corps and the military are a great addition—I have nothing against it at all." Another male officer cited the specific benefits of women in the military as having the military more closely reflect the U.S. population: "I think it's awesome. We are better off as a country when we represent the people that are in it." In addition, according to several of our male Marine Corps officer participants, the female candidates they knew personally were highly motivated and drawn to the Marine Corps for the same reasons as they were themselves: e.g., personal challenge, camaraderie, and the opportunity to serve something greater than themselves.

Negative expressions about women in the military were mentioned in only one of the male focus groups and not mentioned in any of the female focus groups.

With respect to women serving in combat jobs, both men and women expressed positive sentiments.

Interest in Combat Jobs

As shown in Figure 3.1, an overwhelming majority of our female and male focus groups had at least one participant who spoke up and volunteered that they would like to go into combat. However, nearly half of the female enlisted focus groups had at least one person who volunteered that they would prefer not to go into combat.

When we asked recruiters about whether, in their experience, female recruits were interested in entering combat, we saw similar results. In a majority of both our male and female recruiter groups, recruiters stated that some women were interested in combat roles. In more than half of the female recruiter groups, recruiters also stated that some women were not interested in those roles. In contrast to the female groups, however, about a third of the male recruiter groups had someone who stated that women were not interested in those roles.

Comments About Opening up Combat Jobs to Women

Just as male officer and enlisted participants were generally supportive of women in the military, they were also generally supportive of opening up combat jobs to women. Some expressed unqualified support (e.g., "It's great!" or "If males get to, they should too," or "If a woman wants to get out there, no reason to turn away an extra hand"), while others expressed a more neutral type of support. For example, many stated that they were in favor of having women serving in combat long as women were qualified to do the job (e.g, "If they can make it through the training then I'd be happy to serve with them," "If they can do their job, I can respect it," "If they can hold their own"). Some went a bit further and noted that it should be a right afforded to women ("As long as they pass the physical requirement I think they have a right to," "If they prove they can do it, of course they should be able to"). One even implied that qualifications should matter for men, too:

> If a woman performs the same way as a man, it doesn't matter. But I've seen guys that are slower than my mother, so it's not a gender thing.

In addition to the positive and neutral statements, we also heard a few mixed opinions about the involvement of women in combat, with one participant calling it "more of a gray area."

Women expressed similar sentiments: "People should have a right to do what they feel like they should do for their country," "They shouldn't be banned," "I think it's great. We have equal rights to be out there with them. It should be equal." In addition, some expressed a willingness to go into combat if need be. For example, one said:

> Being in SF [Security Forces] it could affect us, we could be pulled to do more, and if they want me to do combat, I am ready. I don't have any hard feelings about that.

Others (in nearly every group there was at least one or two, and sometimes more) said they were excited about the opportunity because they really wanted to go into combat jobs.

To explore the amount of support for the policy change across our groups, we coded the total number of enlisted focus groups where either positive comments or neutral statements of support were expressed. This occurred in all but one of the female and all but two of the male focus groups. In the female group in which no neutral or positive comment was made, the question was not directly asked. In the two male groups, participants in one group simply chose not to speak up on the topic, and in the other group, the question was not directly asked. In addition, in most groups, multiple individuals spoke up and echoed the positive or neutral attitudes made by others, and there were many nods by others in the groups when people were making these types of comments.

Although men and women made many of the same types of positive and neutral comments, we did observe two notable differences. The enlisted male focus groups mentioned the importance of meeting standards for combat positions in their responses far more often than the female focus groups. Very few of the female enlisted focus groups added that point. In other words, the female focus groups tended to express positive sentiments about the move to open up combat jobs to women (e.g., "I think it's great" and "They shouldn't be banned"), whereas the male groups tended to express more neutral stances (e.g., "I'm not opposed" and "As long as they pass the physical requirement").

Despite these differences, our general overall impression from the groups is that there is not a lot of opposition to the policy change in either the male or female focus groups. Many participants were either supportive or neutral on the issue. However, they did acknowledge that there may be some issues of concern. These are discussed in the next section.

Concerns About Women in Combat

Although many of the male participant comments about standards were made in neutral support of the policy (i.e., as long as they can meet the standards, it is fine), some male participants also expressed concerns about the possibility of lowered standards. For example, one male enlisted recruit said:

> If they can do the exact physical things we do, like push-ups, sit-ups, whatever, in a way as a man. Then that's different because then they did it the same as others did it . . . in some cases they tend to give them a little bit of slack because of their size and weight and because they're female, then that's just what kind of worries me.

Another stated: "I just hope they don't lower the standards."

This concern about unequal standards was raised in a number of ways in several of the male recruit focus groups and in one of the female recruit focus groups. In the male recruit groups, the following additional comments were made on the issue:

> If a female can perform at the same level of guys, I don't have a problem. If the Army has different physical standards then . . .

> The women failed three or five times in the Ranger school, but if they were male, they would have taken them out. The males you fail once and you are out. They should be held to the same standards.

> As long as the politics don't come into play, as long as like, standards don't change I think in the same past five years that's fine you have to adjust and like, measure things out so they can be in because they weigh less or, I wouldn't care so much, then that becomes an issue then keep the same don't [unintelligible] the lines just keep it as it was.

> I know that in like some cases where like in pushups, they don't have to hit as much a region that we do for passing, I know it's like for males 17–21, I think its 71 pushups, you need a 100, but I think it's a little bit different with females, it's a little bit lowered and see that's the thing I don't like 'cause they lower things for them so they can pass it or help them make it a little bit easier but I think it should all be the same.

> As long as everyone's meeting the same requirements. As long as the same standards are being upheld. As long as everyone can qualify and we have the same standards in place.

> I heard somewhere if you are going PJ [pararescue jumper] you have to take a physical ability test. I read somewhere that they are going to lower the standards for women with the physical ability test. I don't think they should do that. If they are going through the same training as men they should meet the same requirements.

> Especially for those kinds of jobs. For basic training, it might be different, but if you are going to be a SEAL, [pararescue jumper], Ranger, you should be able to do the same.

> I was just saying keep the requirements the same because when you are out there you can't be worrying about someone else.

> Except for like Marine Corps, those women have the same standards as men, I think if they have the same standards and they pass every test just like men, like physically wise, by all means go for it, but I mean, the Army doesn't have the same physical standards [for women] as [they do for] men. Marine Corps girls are a whole other level. I think to go into Basic they need to do like three pushups I think it was.

In the female recruit group, the following comment was made:

> I'm going to try to do [a special forces combat job] after they open it. I think women should be able to be in special forces but they should have to pass the same standards. Some women think it should be different.

Female officers also expressed some concerns about women in the military being fewer in number compared to men. Said one woman of her experience as an enlisted Marine: "I was the only female in my unit and I felt like I was always out of the loop. They had me in separate bunking with people from other units. So unless communication is improved, I think 'no' [to women in combat]."

Besides meeting standards, recruits raised a few other concerns about women in combat, although these were expressed in far fewer focus groups. For instance, enlisted recruits of both genders proposed a hypothetical combat scenario in which a servicemember might be forced to choose to help either a male or a female servicemember. One male recruit said, "If both a man and a woman get shot at the same time, I'd go for the female."

Male officers also raised concerns about disrupting unit cohesion and, as with a few enlisted recruits, the possibility of combat situations where "you are hurt and a woman is hurt, I would go for her first and save her." In addition, political correctness was raised by one officer: According to him, the infantry constituted a special case that would need to be protected from irresponsible attempts at "using the military as a political playground" in order to maintain infantry's ability to perform critical missions. He noted that women had performed well in specialties other than infantry (e.g., field artillery), but he feared that standards might be lowered for the sake of "political correctness." He believed that the infantry's high-stress environment needed to remain unchanged: "The infantry seems to be an environment where you put people in a really high stress, rigorous, primal environment for a long time. If you put women in a pretty jockish unit, it will do weird things. It will change the entire sociology of it."

While most concerns about women entering combat arose in male focus groups, some women described concerns about women's abilities to perform in those situations, such as carrying men if needed. For instance, one female officer was unsure about combat because "I recognize my limitations. I wouldn't want to hold back a team. It's life or death out there." A female enlisted recruit echoed those concerns about physical performance but noted that women could contribute in multiple ways: "We're all small ladies, so I can see it being an issue trying to carry packs as heavy as us. But they need to figure out where our strong suits could be in combat. For example, I know tanks are really small spaces, so that would be the perfect thing for a woman."

Perceived Benefits of Women in Combat

Despite the concerns they raised about women in combat roles, many also saw potential benefits to it. Some female recruits cited the added opportunity that newly opened combat positions would afford, benefiting their careers. A number of female recruits were specifically interested in choosing a career path based on combat roles. One woman said, "I think it will help your career—it opens up other positions for you to get."

Officers of both genders also pointed out cultural advantages of involving women in combat roles, such as the ability to relate to and speak with foreign national women. One female officer said that if women were not allowed to serve among foreign populations, "culturally you're ostracizing the people you're trying to win over. If women aren't in Afghanistan, you lose a whole side of intelligence [because men would be less able to talk to women and children]."

Key Findings

- Most of our female enlisted focus groups had at least one participant who said they would like to go into a combat job.
- Many male participants reported feeling that women should be allowed into combat if they can meet the same standards as men.
- Some concerns about opening up combat jobs to women were expressed, including that some women might not be able to handle the physical requirements, standards might be lowered, and unit cohesion might be disrupted.

CHAPTER FOUR

Influences on Joining the Military

When deciding whether or not to join the military, potential recruits may consider a number of factors, including perceptions of the benefits of military service, desired career paths, and potential concerns. In addition, this decisionmaking is likely to include the input of key influencers—that is, those who have an impact on recruits' decision to join the military. This group may include close family members (e.g., parents, grandparents, siblings) or community members (peers, teachers, coaches, counselors, scout leaders, or other community leaders). In this chapter we explore the various types of factors that were identified by our participants as possibly influential in a recruit's decision to join the military. We also discuss the perceived role of opening up combat jobs to women and sexual harassment and assault as influencers.

Both recruits and recruiters were asked questions that led to insights related to the topics discussed in this chapter. As such, insights from both groups are discussed below.

Perceived Impact of Allowing Women in Combat on Decisions to Join

We asked recent recruits about whether the policy change to integrate women into combat positions had influenced their decision to join, and whether they thought it would impact their careers. In response, many recruits reported that these views had little impact on their decision to join, and many viewed women in the military as broadly positive.

Enlisted recruits in about half of the male and female focus groups said that *the role of women in general* in the military did not factor into their decision to join. In addition, female recruits in some of the female enlisted focus groups said that the *policy change to open combat jobs to women* did not influence their decision to join. Additionally, in half of the female enlisted focus groups, recruits said they had *no concerns about serving in a majority male organization.* However, other female recruits (about half of female focus groups) said that the *role of women in the military (in general)* did play a role in their decisionmaking.[1] For these recruits, having women more involved in the military—particularly in combat positions—was an attraction. One woman said that the role of women in the military was an appealing influence on her decision to join: "I feel like I'm taking one step toward making women not a minority."

It also appeared that the women-in-combat policy change had little impact on willingness to join among men. In many of the male enlisted focus groups, participants stated that the policy change had not affected their decision to join.

---

[1] In nearly half of the female enlisted focus groups, someone responded no to this question, and in nearly half someone responded yes. In a few groups, participants were vague in their responses, so we did not code the group as responding as either a yes or a no.

Some recruits of both genders thought that the policy change might increase the appeal of military service for both men and women. According to one female enlisted recruit: "If [the ban on women in combat roles] is the reason why women aren't joining, that [the repeal of the ban] will cause them to join." Another female recruit suggested that women who "prove people wrong" by successfully working in combat roles could "influence more females to try out for it." One male officer believed that increased presence of women in the military could drive additional interest from men; "It might light a fire under them, make them want to join it more—'if she can do it, I can do it.' I think you would get more applicants, period."

We also asked recruits what impact they thought the policy change would have on their careers. Women were fairly positive about the policy change, saying they thought it would provide more opportunities and was generally inspiring (e.g., "It presented a challenge and I absolutely love it"). Men generally felt it would have no major impact. In about half of the male enlisted focus groups, someone answered this question by saying it would have no impact, and in nearly every case, multiple people around the room nodded or offered statements of agreement. In the remaining half, the responses varied. In three of those groups, responses were not directly related to the question at hand because the topic of conversation had shifted to other things. In one group, participants chose not to answer the questions about women in combat at all, and as a result were not asked that question as a follow-up. The remaining three groups' responses were as follows:

- In one group, someone said "I think it will change it. It will be different than how it was. It is just going to be different than how it was," without specifying further.
- In a second group, someone responded by stating again that "As long as they get the job done, I don't see how it would interfere."
- In a third group, someone mentioned added competition for jobs.

This last point about a possible lack of jobs was also raised in another one of the groups in which others said there would be no impact. And comments akin to "If standards were lowered, it might be a problem if they cannot do the job" were also mentioned as follow-on comments in two other groups where participants said there would be no impact.

Asked whether the policy change would affect their careers, female officers also listed a few concerns. The first was about the heightened scrutiny that would accompany women in combat roles. One woman mentioned that being "paraded around" in the media could prevent women from being able to "make the difference you could in other roles." Second, multiple female officers mentioned "pressure" on women to perform in combat roles, even in their decision whether or not to enter those specialties. Some envisioned being constantly asked whether they would enter combat roles: "For any minority group, it feels like you need to take advantage of it or you're letting other people in the group down." In addition, pressure to perform could be limiting: "By opening it up, it will also cause undue pressure on females who already can't meet standards. It's hard enough to make the standards already. It's going to make women seem crappier than they already do." Finally, pressure from men to perform "as well as they do" could "create a bigger divide between men and women," leading to resentment.

We asked recruiters about recruits' perceptions on the policy change, and about their own views on how the policy change might impact recruiting. Recruiters in roughly half of the male and half of the female focus groups said that the policy change would not have any impact on their ability to recruit. Some voiced concerns about the potential burdens of having to meet gender targets, while others felt that it would make their jobs easier (e.g., "just more options," "We want more options every day," "If we can put them in more markets, it can only help us—right?") When asked about the policy change's specific impact on recruiting either men or women, few recruiters believed there would be any impact on either. For instance, some recruiters mentioned that the female youth they had spoken with were not typically interested in combat specialties (e.g., "Maybe one in five [women]," "We haven't seen a huge interest in special ops").

Recruits' Concerns About Sexual Harassment and Sexual Assault

We did not explicitly ask about sexual harassment/assault during our recruit focus groups;[2] however, we were still interested in whether it would be among the issues listed when we asked them to recall their concerns prior to joining. In general, female recruits in our enlisted recruit focus groups did not include it in their list of concerns. Nevertheless, the topic did come up in many of the female focus groups in other ways (for example, half of the female groups listed it when we asked what influencers were concerned about). When it was raised, we asked about it. In two of the female focus groups, female recruits stated that they were not worried about it. Others mentioned concerns but said they had found ways to mitigate them. Some female recruits pointed to the "buddy system" as a mechanism for avoiding sexual assault or harassment or the military's emphasis on protocols and training (discussed in one of the female focus groups), and suggested that the possibility of sexual assault or harassment was similar to that in other circumstances (discussed in some of female focus groups). A typical expression of this belief: "It can happen anywhere. Sexual harassment doesn't just happen in the military." We also heard similar beliefs from female officers (e.g., "It happens everywhere"). In contrast, recruits in one of the female focus groups said they had been worried about sexual assault or harassment. We note that these female recruits' views do not necessarily reflect what women who may be considering joining the military perceive about sexual assault and harassment.

Recruits also noted that training of sexual assault prevention and response, however, may at times be overemphasized. In two of the female enlisted focus groups, a recruit mentioned that she had not been concerned about sexual assault or harassment, but it was mentioned so many times that it became a concern as a result. For example, one recruit said:

> Originally no [I wasn't concerned], but when I was going through MEPS [the Military Entrance Processing Station], [recruiters] were talking a lot about sexual harassment and you see the post everywhere and the pictures, this that and the other, so like, I've heard about things that have happened . . . seeing how much it's brought up while enlisting it kinda concerns me a little bit, just because I'm like am I gonna have to fight someone off of me or something like that? . . . I haven't heard anyone have that problem but it just became more real, it's like, keep seeing it so much and being talked about on base it's a concern.

---

[2] The services asked us to not bring up sexual assault or sexual harassment as a discussion topic out of concern that it might raise this as a new concern for some recruits and lead them to rethink their decision to join. We therefore did not raise the issue ourselves in the discussion. Participants in many of the groups (especially the female groups), however, did raise the issue on their own in response to various other questions we asked. As a result, it is worth noting that we cannot know whether responses would have been different if we directly asked about the topic; however, we still view the information gleaned from the spontaneous discussion as useful insights into recruit perspectives on the topics.

Unlike with recruits, we did explicitly prompt recruiters to talk about sexual assault and harassment. When asked, some indicated that they believed it is a concern for some women, whereas others indicated that, in their experience, women are not particularly worried about it. We also followed up by asking how they address the issue if recruits express concerns. In response, in many of the groups recruiters mentioned that they emphasized military protocols, training, and structure. The recruiters also reported reminding recruits that sexual assault and harassment was not a concern that was specific to the military. As one recruiter explained:

> The shy timid females come in and ask about the sexual harassment—"Oh, I read on the news . . ."; then you explain the different programs in place to oppose/combat sexual harassment. Horror stories can be posted online. They reassure them that in . . . college the chance of sexual harassment is just as high, convince them we are a big family and we take care of each other. They get kicked out of the Navy and don't get any second chances.

According to another recruiter:

> Yes, I think a lot of times they see what's in the media, and that shapes perception. I haven't experienced it, but any time I did, the Marines was always digging into it, so I worked hand in hand with sexual response coordinator. No questions about what the proper steps were—it was instant. I also know that universities and colleges don't have to report the way that we do. There's a higher chance of not being reported on a college campus. As a person who has seen the big picture, I'm able to dispel the concerns they see in the media [about the military].

Influencers' Concerns About Sexual Harassment and Sexual Assault

As described above, many female recruits in our focus groups expressed relatively little concern about sexual assault or harassment in the military. However, many recruits as well as recruiters said that this was a concern for recruits' influencers.

In about half of the female new recruit focus groups, recruits mentioned that at least one influencer was concerned about sexual assault or harassment. Parents were concerned for their daughters (e.g., "Mostly because of rape, they picture . . . a little girl in the pit of men," or "My mom was worried about how women are treated in the Marine Corps"). Some recruits also reported that other influencers expressed similar concerns. One female recruit reported, "My boyfriend tried to talk me out of it—said [there is] lots of sexual harassment in the military. '[They are] not going to treat you the same.'" Said another female recruit: "My sisters were concerned. When I told her [one sister] I was joining, the first thing she said was about the sexual harassment. But I told them it could happen anywhere, inside or outside the military." According to another female recruit: "My grandma was mostly focused on the bad, like I'll get raped or something."

Recruiters of both genders mentioned that influencers had expressed concerns about sexual assault or harassment in the military that recruiters needed to address (this was mentioned in about half of the groups). One recruiter said, "With women, the parents are the gatekeepers. Whatever the parents say goes. Parents are concerned about combat for women. Going to war, the general idea of combat and war and sexual harassment is an issue . . . but not specifically related to this policy." Another recruiter said:

> Usually the father is freaking out but the mother is just worried. Sexual harassment and sexual assault they [the military] train for it almost every week. It's a no-no. They [the military] have policies that state all the things that will happen if you do it. Can't say 100 percent whether it's going to happen. We train to get everybody involved. If someone touches someone, they are trained to intervene. They [the military] explain the policies. Tell them about the procedures, how the investigation goes down, informal, formal, etc.

Recruiters as Influencers

Enlisted recruits described somewhat mixed reactions to their experiences with recruiters. In most of the enlisted male and female focus groups, recruits said that they appreciated that their recruiter was transparent and honest. Yet some enlisted recruits (albeit far fewer) also mentioned a number of less positive aspects of their recruiting experience. A few recruits stated that they would have preferred that their recruiters had provided an escort to Military Entrance Processing Stations (MEPS). Others felt that their recruiter had pressured them to join, ignored them, or not been totally honest: "They kind of sugarcoat it, but it's their job. Recruits should do their own research to see what's true. I would go and watch videos and see it was different from what I heard." Several recruits said that the recruiter for their branch of service had been honest or did not pressure them to join, unlike in their experiences with recruiters from other branches. Finally, some enlisted recruits described recruiting issues that echoed recruiters' concerns about lack of female recruiters and insufficient recruiting time. For some female recruits, conversations with male recruiters about "female questions" were awkward. Another recruit mentioned having called multiple recruiters and recruiting offices, but "only one picked up [the phone]. No one else responded."

On the whole, the officers in our focus groups described very positive experiences with recruiters. For instance, respondents said that recruiters had "done everything possible for me" and "didn't treat you like a number." They also appreciated when recruiters explained the reasoning behind why they would "make you do something," such as creating high-stress situations: to "make you think on your feet." Several officers praised recruiters' efforts to prepare them mentally and physically, describing recruiter-organized physical training sessions as "a great resource to prepare us for when are there." One such response mentioned "how helpful, and their sense of responsibility to get us prepared and foster leadership in us and interact. I couldn't have asked for more." They reported having such a positive experience with the recruiters that they frequently sought out them out, entering the recruiting stations of their own accord.

Unsurprisingly, officer recruits reported looking to their recruiters as role models. One recruit saw that his recruiters "held themselves to a high standard, and that always stuck with me." However, there was one less-than-positive experience with a former recruiter, described as "pulling teeth." This recruit opted to start the recruiting process with a different service (one he was less interested in), and only returned to his service of choice once a new recruiter arrived.

Importance of Female Recruiters and Female Events

Some female recruits in our focus groups stated that they greatly appreciated what female recruiters were able to do for them, such as being able to answer what they called "female questions," holding all-female events in the DEP, and bringing in female active-duty servicemembers for individual meetings. Figure 4.1 shows the percent of recent recruit focus groups in which female recruiter–related themes were mentioned in response to our questions. For instance, when asked what they would recommend to attract more women to join, recruits in many of the female enlisted focus groups suggested "more female recruiters." This was unsurprising, given that many female recruits also mentioned that they liked having all-female events and when female recruiters or other active-duty women were available to answer their questions. One female new recruit said, "For females, it's kind of awkward talking to a man about female problems." Another said, "When you first step into a recruiting office and you see only male recruiters, but you have questions about female problems, you can't really open that conversation up with a man." Another recalled that when military recruiters came to talk to the students in high school, there was a representative from each service—but they were all male. They held a pull-up contest, which the boys appeared to love, but it made her feel awkward since pull-ups were not something she regularly practiced. As a result, she did not feel comfortable talking to any of them at the time. Instead, the first time she talked to a recruiter was at a recruiting office after she had graduated. She said that while she understood that it would be hard to have a female representative for every service (because women are so underrepresented), if at least one of the four representatives had been female, she would have felt more comfortable.

Recruiters' perspectives and experiences mirrored those of the new recruits. One male recruiter said:

Figure 4.1.
Female Enlisted Recruit Focus Group Responses: Preferences for Female Recruiters and Female Events

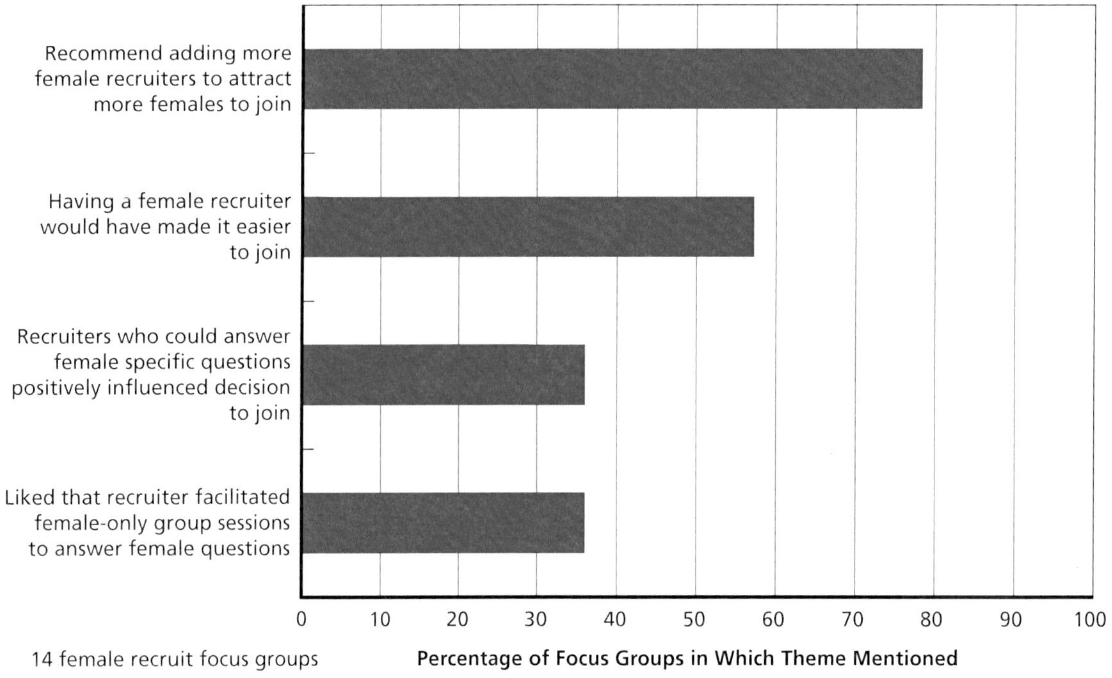

RAND *RR1538-4.1*

> Any female may take her [female recruiter] words over mine to assure them of what it would be like in the Marine Corps. I was in a combat MOS [military occupational specialty]. I didn't see women a whole lot. When we have female concerns, I push the female recruiter to talk to the females. Having more females out in the street would be beneficial. They seem more open to asking questions with other females.

Female recruiters may play a key role in the recruiting process by building confidence in young female applicants, serving as role models, and answering female-specific questions. Some recruiters mentioned that they organized quarterly all-female DEP meetings to enable women to "relax and ask personal questions." In these meetings, recruits asked a range of questions about expectations for dress (e.g., uniform, hair, nails), feminine hygiene questions (e.g., showers, birth control, menstruation), and children (e.g., childcare, schooling). Other female recruiters reported bringing in recent recruits who had just completed initial training to allow women in the DEP to ask questions about what to expect.

When asked for suggestions to improve recruiting, many female recruiters said that more female recruiters would be helpful. Said one female recruiter, "They [male recruiters] do send them [female recruits] to me for certain questions, even if they don't pass them to me . . . If you are a female in recruiting you are in high demand for your entire flight or for your entire city." Another recruiter suggested "increased access to female recruiters . . . by example a person will see who they can be, so the more you show, 'hey, here we are.' If they see us more, hear of us more, interact with us more, they will think, 'hey, I can do that'. . . so why not be GI Jane?"

Key Findings

- The policy change to allow women in combat did not appear to be a strong negative influence on joining the military for our recruit participants. Many male recruits in our focus groups reported that their decision to join was not affected by the policy change. Many of the women saw it as a positive.
- Neither women in combat nor sexual assault and harassment appeared to be strong influences on recruits' decision to join the military.
- Many female recruits in our focus groups reported not being concerned about sexual assault or harassment in the military, and that they had found ways to mitigate what concerns they did have.
- Many recruiters in our focus groups are also not concerned about the policy change's impact on recruiting.
- Recruiters appear to be important influencers in recruit decisions, and recruits expressed having both positive and negative experiences with recruiters.
- Many female recruits in our focus groups prefer female recruiters for their ability to address female-specific questions.
- Influencers are more likely to be concerned about sexual assault or harassment than the female recruits themselves.

CHAPTER FIVE

Recruiting Policies and Strategies

While Title 10 of the U.S. Code is the main governing source of recruiting policy, the individual services also establish policy and guidance for recruiters, such as accession targets (e.g., gender, skills, education) and eligibility requirements. The recruiting process typically begins with contact between the potential recruit and a local recruiter, although contact methods may differ. For instance, recruits with high propensity to join may actively seek out recruiters, but recruiters will also reach out to local youth. Potential recruits are initially screened by the recruiters for eligibility and then are scheduled for a visit to the MEPS for additional testing and screening. If qualified, the recruit will then sign an enlistment contract. They may be sent to initial training or placed into DEP for up to two years before finally entering active duty (10 U.S.C. 515). While in the DEP, the recruit is part of the Inactive Ready Reserve.

We asked recruiters and leaders of the recruiting services about their views on the recruiting environment, policies and strategies for recruiting women, and whether recruiting approaches had changed in response to issues such as women in combat or sexual harassment and assault. Their responses are summarized in this chapter. Although we did not explicitly ask recruits about recruiting policies and procedures, they did offer insights into the need for increased efficiencies in the recruiting process and the importance of addressing misperceptions about military service. As a result, in the sections that follow, we also present insights gleaned from the recruit discussions.

Findings from the Recruiter and Recruit Discussions

Figures 5.1 and 5.2 address recruiters and recruits' ideas about improving the recruiting process.

Processing Efficiencies and Improvements to Materials Used in Recruiting

Both recruiters and recruits report dissatisfaction with what they view as burdensome administrative requirements, which included onerous paperwork, multiple versions of the same form, systems that did not "talk to one another," long wait times due to MEPS inefficiencies, and the requirement to account for recruiters' time in detail. For instance, seemingly avoidable wait times were a common theme. According to one recruit: "To speak to a counselor, it took eight hours. I was pretty much sitting there for eight hours. I don't think it should take that long." Another recruit said, "If my recruiter goes somewhere else, the other recruiter doesn't have access to my files. So I have to wait, I'm stuck. Hand off to another recruiter."

Many recruits referenced lack of efficiency at MEPS visits: "Someone down the hall will have the exact same copy of paperwork and won't be able to communicate at all. None of it is

Figure 5.1
Recruiter Focus Group Responses: Improving Recruiting Process

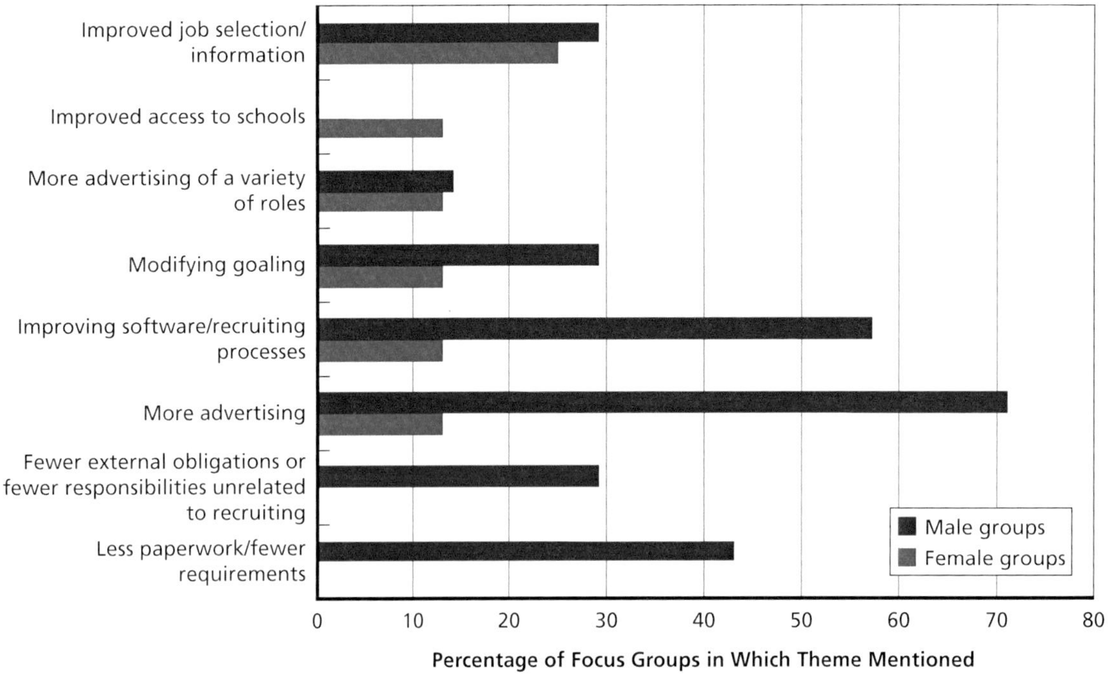

RAND *RR1538-5.1*

Figure 5.2
Enlisted Recruit Focus Group Responses: Improving Recruiting Process

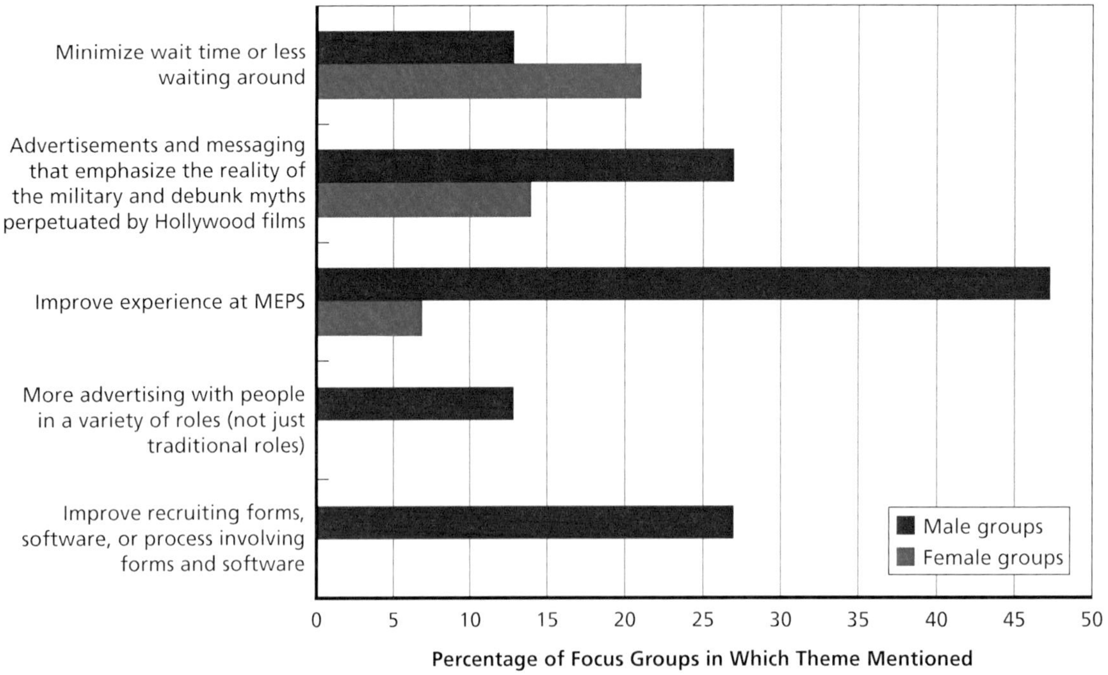

RAND *RR1538-5.2*

connected, none on the same page with each other. It's a mess." These inefficiencies frustrated recruits and recruiters alike.

Some recruiters suggested that bureaucratic processes, by extending the time needed to complete applications ("bureaucratic red tape slows down the recruiting process tenfold"), contributed to losing applicants. One recruiter said:

> At our particular station, we've lost people waiting for waivers on dependency, physical waivers, medical waivers, DUI [driving under the influence] waivers, we've lost people for all of these things. When all it is, is paperwork. Someone's got to sign it, take however long you think you need to take, OK, 30 days, cool. We could sacrifice that amount of time, cause then we could tell someone something tangible. Hey, I appreciate you starting the process with us in June, we'll have an answer for you by July. Hey, I appreciate you starting the process with me in February, it's October 2015, I might have an answer for you in January 2016. I actually have a person I've been working with since February who I have no answers for, because I'm waiting for a medical waiver to come back.

Some recruiters also felt that reducing administrative requirements could improve recruiting. They thought that having more time to spend out prospecting would make their jobs easier, rather than having to account in detail for their time, complete surveys, or other unrelated obligations.

Addressing Misperceptions About the Military

Several recruits in our focus groups described common misperceptions about military service as an issue in recruiting both more men and more women. Countering these perceptions, they suggested, could help attract more people to consider joining the military. As shown in Figure 5.2, some of the female and the male enlisted focus groups recommended more advertisements or other messaging that would emphasize the reality of the military—for instance, debunking myths perpetuated in movies. Several recruits mentioned that they knew people whose image of the military involved only infantry, or being deployed and going to war. Said one recruit: "They all think if you join the military you're going to go to Iraq, you're going to just go out there and shoot." Another recruit suggested the need to "get rid of the misconceptions. It's not about being all gung-ho." Recruits also believed that some saw the military as merely a fallback option: "The image you get is that you go into the military because have nothing else to do with your life."

To increase women's interest in military service, recruits suggested the specific need to address misconceptions about the role of women in the military. In about half of the female enlisted focus groups, female recruits recommended more advertising featuring women in a variety of roles as a way to attract more women to join. According to one female recruit:

> In my mind, [the military] meant "guys serving in war." That's what a lot of people think, not that [the military] is for women. So if it was shown more that it is for women, like advertising, [it could] change the cloud over everyone's head.

One female enlisted recruit described the advertising she had seen as not appealing to women: "All the posters have males in them, and they're always talking about brotherhood." Another female recruit said, "Look at START [Standards, Transition, Acknowledgement, Requirements, Training] guide, you see women on the cover. They're trying to show diversity, and I think Navy is doing a good job of that. I look at other services (like Marines), [they're trying to be more macho]."

Officer participants of both genders suggested that advertising could help provide female role models, such as commercials depicting women in leadership roles. Some of the female officers believed that for women to see these role models would be "empowering." Said one: "Aspirations are the biggest thing." Another suggestion was for role models that would be more directly available ("definitely more mentors").

Some of the female officer participants also suggested addressing stigma, noting that women in the military might have a negative image. According to one female officer, "Most women don't see themselves in the military. There's a stigma." In contrast, she "loved" seeing a female high-ranking officer. "There's nothing better than that . . . it gives you something to strive for—it's super empowering." To address this, one suggestion was for advertising to show that women in the military "don't have to be butch." Discussing among themselves, two female officers pointed out that there were different ways to be a woman in the military. According to one, "They should inspire women to empower themselves. Show that girls can be tough." In response, another respondent said: "But I also think if a girl wants to be dainty and be in the military, that's okay too."

Some officer recruits also suggested that it would help to emphasize the flexible possibilities of military service. One male officer, asked what might help recruit his peers, mentioned that "A lot of my friends were not aware that this was not a life commitment. They didn't realize it was only a short contract; you aren't committing to forever." A female officer echoed this lack of understanding of the military as a career, noting that many of her friends wanted to go into nursing, but "They don't realize you can do it here too, not just in a hospital. And it doesn't mean you can't have a family or you can't settle down." Some female officer participants also suggested "emphasizing the occupation" because women might not be aware of specific opportunities for them in the military ("I didn't even know women could join the Marines at first").

As shown in Figure 5.3, recruiters expressed very similar ideas when it came to ways to interest more women in military service. Recruiters were not explicitly asked about ways to improve interest across both genders.

Disincentives for Recruiting Women

As shown in Figure 5.4, some recruiters explicitly target women, others do not; some use a different approach when recruiting women, and others do not. One disincentive toward recruiting women came up in nearly half of the male recruiter groups: Some men believed recruiting women was particularly difficult for male recruiters because of the possibility that their actions might be misconstrued.

Many male recruiters felt that they were often perceived negatively when prospecting, such as when approaching female youth in public places: "You feel like a creeper walking up if you don't have a female recruiter . . . the first thing [female recruits] think is they are being hit on." They also noted similar issues when calling female recruits ("Just because you are a male calling a 17-year-old female, parents get concerns. It's a big obstacle") or visiting female recruits at home. These concerns extended throughout the recruiting process, leading recruiters to avoid driving alone with a recruit of the opposite gender, or being alone in a recruiting office: "I have a female in my office . . . I told her if she is uncomfortable, we can call your dad or take my computer outside." Another recruiter suggested that being alone with a recruit

Figure 5.3
Recruiter Focus Group Responses: Ideas About How to Attract More Women to the Military

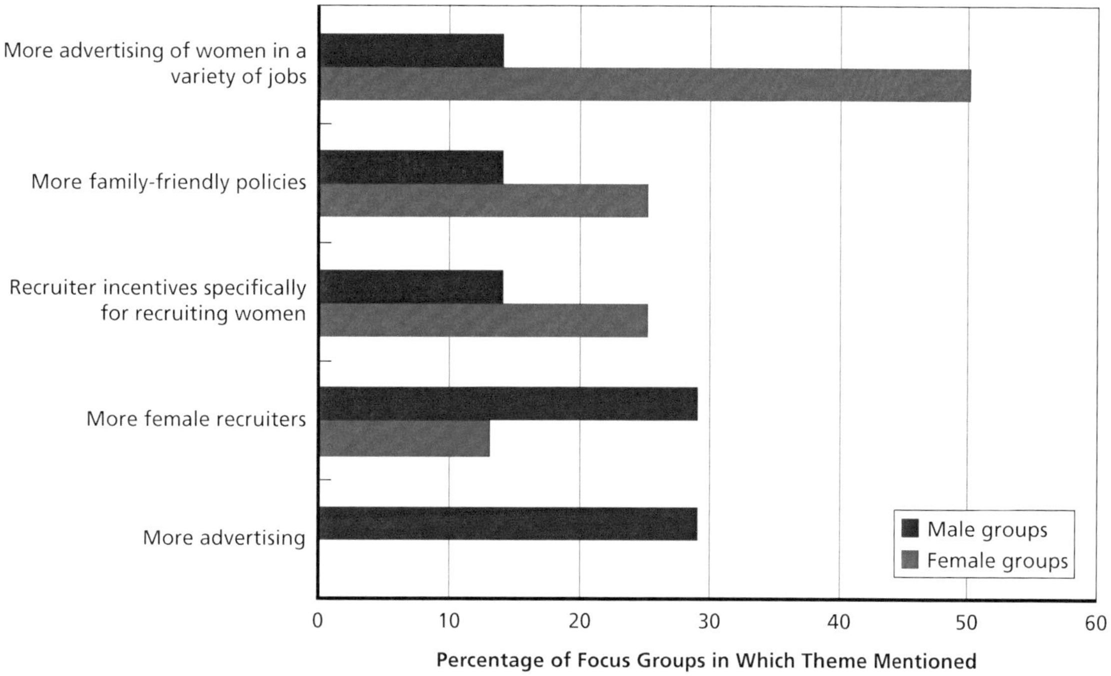

RAND *RR1538-5.3*

Figure 5.4
Recruiter Focus Group Responses: Incentives and Approaches to Recruiting Women

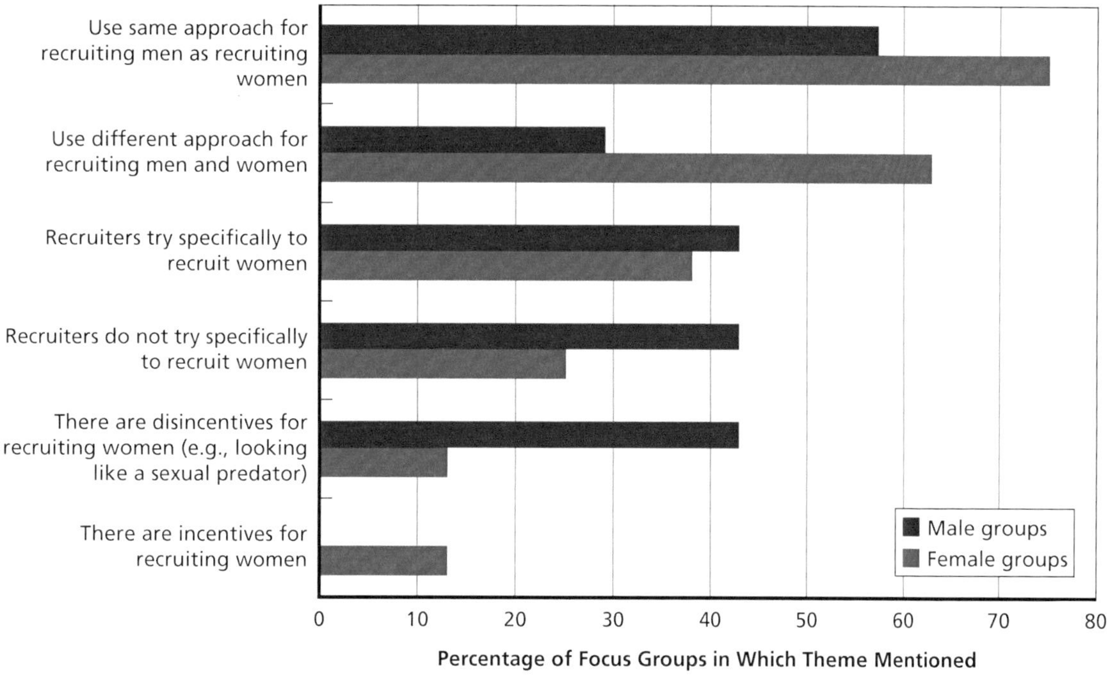

RAND *RR1538-5.4*

could lead others to draw erroneous conclusions, such as if a female recruit was upset for an innocuous reason: "Everything could be 100-percent fine [and then] some passerby may see a female going in there [the recruiter's office] . . . The blinds are already semi-shut . . . she's [actually] sad because she did bad on the test." Consequently, male recruiters may hesitate to seek female recruits:

> I'm a little reluctant to find females. I'm a little hesitant, and I'm not going to do it by myself. And if I'm alone, and I find myself alone, I'm out. I'm running. I'm not going to be found alone with a female, that's another obstacle we have to get over.

Some recruiters expressed specific concerns about potential consequences of sexual misconduct allegations: "Anything can be made up. Males and females—all it takes is one allegation and you are kicked out of recruiting and you are out." One recruiter perceived a lack of support if this were to occur: "We are expendable . . . it's very risky. It can put a horrible dent in your career." As a result, male recruiters in our focus groups perceived disincentives that could lead other recruiters to not recruit women:

> I could imagine some recruiters are probably intimidated or don't want to recruit for females just because of how strict recruiting policies are when it comes to recruiter to applicant, and being [a] different sex. I'm sure there's some out there that are just like, I don't even want to get caught up, cause you can't transport them in a vehicle by yourself, and you can't interview them by yourself, it's always got to be a buddy system. So I could imagine there's probably recruiters out there that don't even want to get involved, so they just stay away from trying to recruit females. They just want to prevent any issues with the recruiter, of he said/she said at that point.

As shown in Figure 5.4, people in the male recruiter groups were slightly more likely to say they take the same approach to recruiting women than they were to say they take differing approaches, possibly because of the disincentives they mentioned. One recruiter pointed out that a gender-neutral approach might help reduce the potential for misunderstandings or misperceptions:

> If we try to recruit differently to males than we do females, we eventually hem ourselves up with something that we don't want to be caught up in. Like, "the recruiter came on to me," [because we tried to change our approach. So, keep your approach neutral regardless of what gender you're talking to, regardless of who you're talking to, and you're never going to have a chance of stepping on your own toes.

Male recruiters also mentioned several other ways they try to address these issues, such as by not being alone with a female recruit, or by handing off female recruits to female recruiters. This latter approach may cause additional burden for the few female recruiters, particularly considering that, according to recruiters and leadership, more time is typically needed to recruit women.

Lastly, some recruiters explained that women require more effort to recruit (they are harder to convince to sign, more likely to drop out of DEP before they ship, etc.), which means that given the choice, a male candidate is a better potential lead than a woman. This means some recruiters are more likely to go after the easy targets.

Approaches to Recruiting Women and Addressing Sexual Harassment/Assault Concerns

About half of the female and male recruiter groups stated that referring a recruit to a female recruiter is one effective way to recruit women. Some of the female recruiter groups also mentioned responding to or creating resources pertaining to female-specific questions and emphasizing family-friendly policies as effective ways to recruit women. In addition, both male and female recruiters described their approaches to how to address concerns about sexual harassment/assault. Those are listed in Figure 5.5. Interestingly, the approaches discussed by some of the male recruiters focused largely on approaches for addressing concerns expressed by influencers (such as family), whereas the female groups also discussed approaches to addressing concerns expressed by the applicants.

Findings from the Leadership Discussions

Challenges to Recruiting Women

In response to our questions about their experiences recruiting women, senior leaders described several challenges they faced specifically in recruiting women, including gender differences in propensity. The commander of the Air Force Recruiting Service noted that women may be less likely to choose combat jobs without first seeing successful role models in those same positions. The commanding general of the U.S. Army Recruiting Command described various gender-specific attitudes that could present difficulties in recruiting women, citing JAMRS research as having been useful in drawing these lessons. These included JAMRS findings that, compared with men, women were more risk-averse; less confident they could be successful in the military (including basic training and combat performance); more concerned with injury/death (including psychological trauma) and leaving friends and family; and less likely to perceive that the Army included "people like me." He also mentioned that jobs with "unusual time commitments or long working hours" would give women pause, based on their future plans to have a family. Finally, he stated that although men and women shared many similar concerns, JAMRS research indicated that there were gender differences in "myths" about Army service, such as that anybody joining the Army would immediately see combat or would be psychologically damaged. He noted, "There are literally women in the U.S. today that come in and ask a recruiter if they can have a family and 'Can I get married?'"

Based on these concerns that women hold about the military, recruiters may need to spend more time and effort convincing women to join. The commanding general of the Marine Corps Recruiting Command stated that, over time, the Marine Corps has found that more time is required ("two or three times as much effort") to recruit women, particularly during the interview process: "If it takes two interviews for a man, it takes about six interviews to contract a female. You have to find the time and conduct those interviews. The amount of time is substantially more for a woman than it is for a man. It takes more time to convince them. It takes more time for families to be convinced. It takes them more time to overcome personal doubt on whether or not this is something that they can do." Marine Corps women are also three times as likely than men to drop out during training, due to "injury or failure to adapt, etc." This higher attrition rate means that if recruiters "contract and ship a female and she doesn't make it, [they] have to get that contract back and make it up later on in the year."

Figure 5.5
Recruiter Focus Group Responses: Approaches to Addressing Sexual Harassment/Assault Concerns

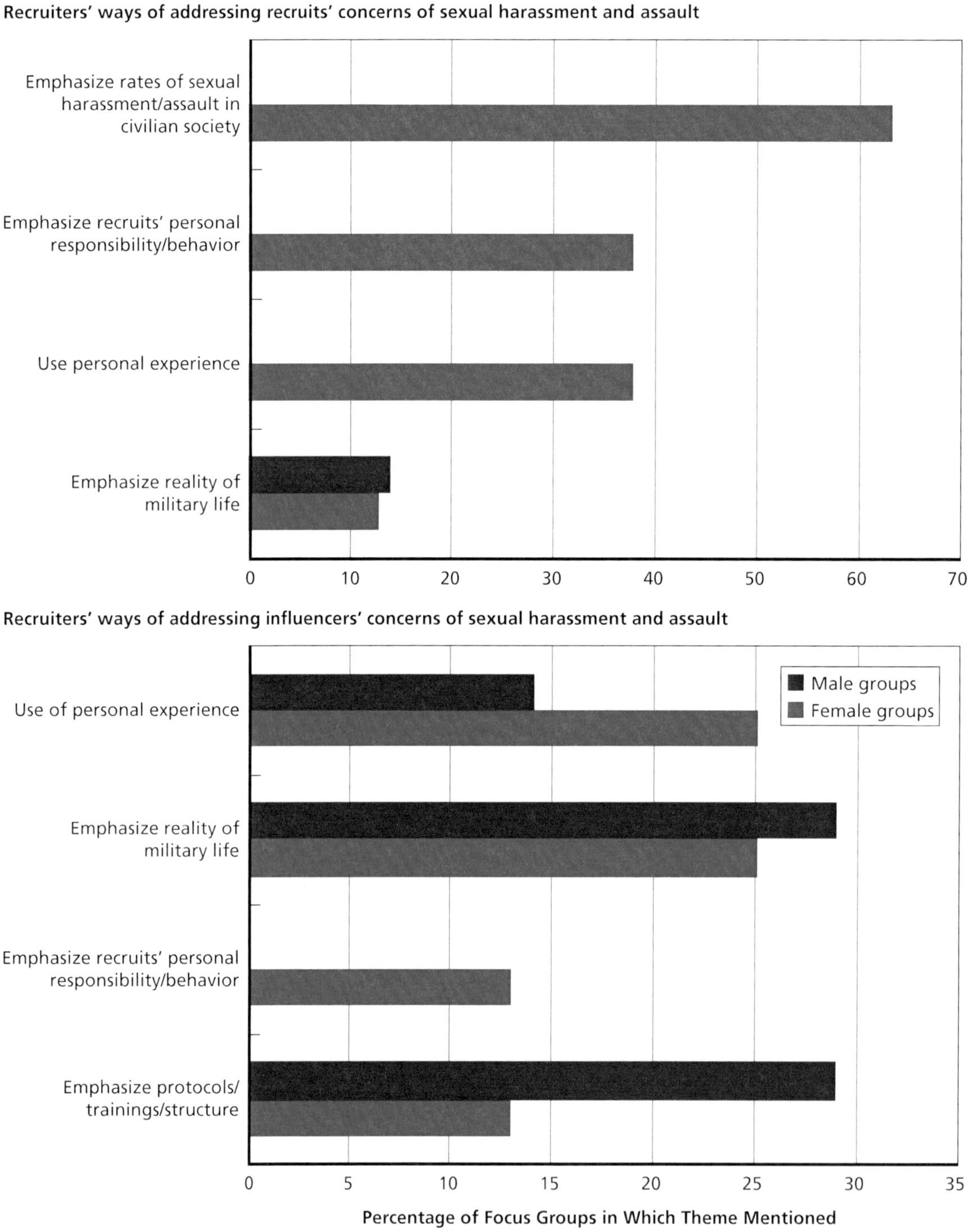

RAND *RR1538-5.5*

Efforts to Engage in Targeted Recruiting of Women

Recruiting leadership from all four services stated very clearly that they are strongly in favor of increased gender diversity. This was a common theme for the four heads of the respective recruiting services. They emphasized a workforce gender mix that more accurately reflected the general population. For instance, the commander of Navy Recruiting Command said that the composition of the Navy should be "more representative of our country and the people who compose our country." The Army commander said, "We want to increase the number of women making the decision to better represent both the Army and the society." However, leadership also generally lamented that they are fighting an uphill battle. For example, according to the Navy's recruiting commander "Everybody is looking for females for all the right reasons . . . Everyone wants diversity in their workforce . . . In order to maintain the competitive edge, we have to get out there."

Yet, although they acknowledge the benefit of increased female representation, the services do not always seek to specifically recruit women. For example, the Marine Corps commander said that the Marine Corps wanted as many women as wanted to join: "If we find more women who want to come, then more women will take their place amongst us in the Marine Corps." Similarly, the Air Force recruiting commander stated that they aim to "get the best [and the] brightest and [then] hope to meet our internal goals [for recruiting women]." The Air Force's overall approach to recruiting is "inspire, engage, and recruit," which is applied equally to men and women. In this approach, the Air Force seeks to present advertising that features women in a variety of roles, so that "young women can see themselves in these roles and opportunities and careers." These "inspire/engage" steps are intended to boost interest that will then help the recruiters to recruit young women. The Army recruiting commander described their approach to recruiting women as a goal, not a requirement: "We see it as . . . the percentage is a good thing, but there isn't anyone coming back to me as the commander saying I didn't meet the goal. Instead, they say we have made our [overall accession] mission but we've fallen short in the Army Reserves, and that's been the case for four years."

Table 5.1 describes each service's general approach to recruiting women, according to these senior recruiting leaders. All the recruiting services have outlined at least some goals, although they differ and are not necessarily requirements. The Army and Marine Corps focus on end strength, while the Air Force and Navy emphasize diversity in the pipeline—applicants and accessions, respectively. The Air Force's focus on applicants is based on their belief that they can encourage and track, but not hire, "based upon race, ethnicity or gender. That's why we have an application goal, not an accession goal." The other services did not mention any restrictions to hiring based on gender. According to the Army recruiting commander, the recruiting goal of 20 percent women is discretionary, rather than a requirement outlined in its annual mission letter that articulates recruiting requirements. The Marine Corps' female mission is evenly divided among recruiting stations and substations across the country, so that each receives its "fair share of requirements."

The services indicated that they were generally meeting targets for recruiting women, with a few exceptions. For instance, the Marine Corps recruiting commander mentioned occasional difficulties in finding sufficient numbers of qualified women, but viewed this more as an issue related to substations' management of shipping flow "rather than the ability to find a female that wants to go into the Marine Corps," To make up for a lack of qualified women, they "rely heavily" on the DEP to help women qualify through "mental, morale, and physical training," although time spent in the DEP also introduces possibilities that they will drop out (e.g., lose interest, get pregnant, get a disqualifying tattoo).

Table 5.1
Service-Specific Goals and Recruiter Incentives for Recruiting Women

Service	Goal	Success at Reaching Goal	Incentives for Goal	Tracking Progress to Goal
Air Force	• No female enlisted goals • 30% female officer applicants	• Close to or exceeding goal (including nonline officers)	No additional incentive for subset of overall goal	Track applications and accessions
Army	• 20% female enlisted	• Most female active duty enlistments in 8 years (fiscal year 2015) • Reserve accessions fell short for past 4 years (fiscal year 2015)	Accessions incentives (e.g., by MOS) established by Department of the Army G-1, but not for recruiting force to recruit specific gender	Track accessions outcomes by race/ethnicity and gender, in conjunction with Army Human Resources Command (HRC) and Department of the Army G1
Marine Corps	• Annual female contracting and shipping missions • Above 10% female end strength by 2021	• Consistently meet shipping targets • In some years miss contracting targets (e.g., 2006)	No separate bonus for recruiting women	Closely track accessions as required for even flow shipping
Navy	• 25% female accessions profile in enlisted force	• Yes, but anticipate future difficulty as requirements increase	Reward high performers, but no additional incentive for subset of overall goal	Automated tools to track contracts, accessions, and shipping

None of the services provide incentives to recruiters specifically for bringing in recruits with gender diversity. The Army provides recruiters with non-gender-specific accessions incentives, such as for certain MOSs. The Navy rewards high-performing recruiters for "good performance across the board," but not for recruiting any particular individuals. Neither the Air Force nor Marine Corps provide recruiter incentives. The Air Force and Navy recruiting commanders asserted that their recruiters were sufficiently motivated without additional incentives.

All the services indicated that they track recruiting outcomes, such as applications and accessions, to monitor progress towards their diversity goals.

Recruiting Changes in Response to Opening of Combat Roles to Women

We asked recruiting leaders about their views of the current recruiting landscape, such as general interest or shifts in recruiting trends related to the policy change to open combat jobs to women. We also asked about any current or planned changes in their recruiting strategies as a result of the policy change (see Table 5.2). Across the interviews, the recruiting leadership expressed general agreement that the policy change would not affect their recruiting strategies or outlook to a great degree, or beyond ongoing efforts. They mentioned that preparations for the policy change were already underway and, in some cases, recruiting changes had already been implemented.

The Army recruiting commander said it was still early to tell about long-term changes, but that based on survey data, the Army had seen little change in interest in combat positions after the policy change in January 2013. The Army has noted that female representation in the Army Reserves was higher than in the active component, possibly owing to migration of support specialties to the reserves. The Army recruiting commander also expressed some optimism that the policy change might constitute at least a slightly positive influence on female recruiting: "Women like the fact that there are more opportunities; the playing field is a bit more level in terms of the things they can do, but [this has not] necessarily translated into more women wanting to join the Special Forces. I think we just have to take a long-term view on this." He stated that they were "committed to enable women to successfully serve in combat roles," and would ensure "conditions are set for their arrival to training" once decisions had been made regarding which combat MOSs would be open to women.

The Marine Corps has undertaken several efforts to prepare for the policy change. Thus far, it has opened 11 MOSs (three officer, eight enlisted) to women and conducted training and put out materials about those jobs. According to the commander:

> [We] interviewed every woman in the DEP so they understand what is available to them in an effort to see if they are interested. We spent a year working on that and contracted 72 females for the new MOSs. In one particular (anti-air defense), we were contracting for land gunners and half of the billets were subscribed by females. That is what we contracted, and there's a difference in contracted to operating force. We are still watching them go through recruit training. We had to curtail it, we had such a response because that 35 represented half of the available spots for the year. Radar operators, we had a number of women contract for that . . . we had less people contact for track vehicle . . . tank mechanics . . . always been a challenge with respect to females. They don't see themselves as able to do it or

Table 5.2
Recruiting Policy Changes in Response to Current Environment by Service

Service	Opening Combat Jobs to Women	Sexual Harassment and Assault in the Military
Air Force	• Produce marketing materials that women can identify with • Modify mobile assets to show female role models (e.g., doing pull-ups) • Marketing shows women participating in activities such as helicopter jumping	• Inspire, Deter, Detect, and Hold Accountable (IV2A) program, provides lessons on professional relationships and conduct
Army	• Working with G1 and HRC to ensure conditions are set for women's arrival into newly opened specialties • Highlight available opportunities to women via marketing/advertising efforts	• SHARP program • Bystander training • Identified certain positions of special trust and authority (PASTA), where individuals identified as most likely to be in contact with the population that are most at risk for sexual assault (ages 18–24), which includes recruiters. There are additional screenings for individuals entering PASTA positions.
Marine Corps	• Developed integrated task force • Trained force to encourage women to consider newly-open MOSs • Interviewed every woman in DEP to ensure they understood available opportunities but without directing into a particular MOS • Issued "training credit" to women who passed training and qualified to enter combat positions	• Two person rule with respect to male recruiters • Detailed campaigns in all six districts • Character training in the DEP • Talking to recruits including a survey of whether they had been a victim of sexual assault prior to enlisting • Programs and counselors ready to meet needs • Published commander's policy regarding concerns of retaliation • Screened recruiters for prior instances of sexual assault • Put best people in recruiting
Navy	• No specific changes; Navy is prepared for incoming special operators	• No specific changes

> they just don't want to turn a wrench. We had some experience; over a year . . . we weren't surprised by the relatively low number.

Through this experience, the Marine Corps found that many people contracted to service were in favor of opening the MOSs, even if they did not express interest: "They voice strongly, but they didn't vote with their feet—they just wanted to support their fellow sisters."

The Air Force commander indicated similar experiences regarding the seven combat Air Force specialties opened to women. These positions were difficult to fill before they were opened to women, and they believed that "nothing really changes for us . . . It's hard to recruit a successful PJ (pararescue jumper), and we don't see any change to that." But "[it won't] take long before we have our first female PJ." The Air Force is making changes to its recruiting tactics, based on the belief that allowing women to see other women in these positions will be important. For instance, the Air Force has modified its mobile recruiting assets (i.e., trucks that appear at events such as state fairs and the Super Bowl) to feature female role models (e.g., female airmen doing pull-ups). It has also produced marketing materials, documenting the experiences of women currently in the training pipeline and creating ads with women diving from helicopters and riding on motorcycles.

The Navy commander said that the Navy was prepared for the policy change and did not plan to make specific changes. In this senior leader's view, the Navy has been consistently gender integrated and would readily receive women in combat jobs:

> It's been there for us the whole way. We have women divers, women [explosive ordnance disposal], women . . . Now we have female air crewman . . . We look at ratings, so diver, [explosive ordnance disposal], air crew rescue swimmers . . . As things are opening up, gets us in the special operations realm . . . I haven't even talked about submarines. [As we] continue on this path, we are ready to accept the folks who come in to be our special operators.

We also asked about potential challenges with recruiting men once the policy change was implemented. None of the services' recruiting leadership expressed concern that the policy change would result in future difficulties. For instance, the Marine Corps recruiting leader said:

> I see no problem with regard to men. We've gone through the repeal of Don't Ask Don't Tell, the integrated task force effort, we are very confident that we are going to find enough men and women of character to take up our challenge to become Marines, that we are going to be okay. Of all the things that I worry about on a regular basis, finding enough men to be Marines is not something I'm concerned with in the economic environment right now.

The Army recruiting leader also did not foresee major challenges recruiting men and, moreover, endorsed ongoing efforts to determine gender-neutral standards by specialty:

> If an individual can meet those requirements regardless of [whether they are] men or women, [the job is] open to them . . . If they can meet the standard they can go into it . . . There is a lot of goodness in it.

Recruiters in our focus group generally did not anticipate changing their recruiting approach as a result of the policy change. A few recruiters emphasized the need to fit recruits' interests and qualifications (e.g., "Everyone comes with their own desires—my job is to help facilitate that desire," or "You don't want to sell spec ops for anyone that is not interested"). However, one recruiter allowed for the possibility that gender targets associated with the policy change could alter her approach to recruiting women: "It will, eventually, if they make it a push. If they throw numbers at it, because that will make life miserable."

Recruiting Changes in Response to Military Sexual Assault

As shown in Table 5.2, we asked the senior leaders to describe recruiting policy changes regarding military sexual harassment and assault. The Army requires additional screening for people (e.g., recruiters) entering "certain positions of special trust and authority," specifically "defining those individuals likely to be involved." This requirement was related to an OUSD/P&R policy change regarding "sensitive positions"—individuals likely to be in contact with people from ages 18–24, who are most at risk for sexual assault. The Army also adheres to other OUSD/P&R-directed sexual assault prevention efforts, such as Sexual Harassment/Assault Response and Prevention (SHARP) and bystander training.

The Marine Corps conducted a coordinated training and monitoring effort that broadly encompassed the recruiting force, including commanders, applicants, and recruits, and that was consistently reinforced. Each of its six recruiting districts developed detailed campaign plans, trained personnel and ensured they met standards set in those plans, and instituted a "two-person rule" for male recruiters to interact with female recruits. The recruits themselves underwent "character training" and discussed sexual harassment and assault with regard to their rights and responsibilities (e.g., reporting any incidents to the closest Marine). Even though those incidents would have occurred outside of the Marine Corps' responsibility, the Marine Corps instituted programs and had counselors meet with recruits at recruiting depots to inquire about whether they were a victim of inappropriate sexual behavior prior to service or had other issues that might require counseling. To address concerns of retaliation, the Marine senior leader published a commander's policy and briefed it at a national training seminar, encouraged reporting of possible retaliation up the chain of command, and attempted to ensure follow-up on individual cases.

The Navy's recruiting commander emphasized zero tolerance within the Navy for sexual harassment and assault, pointing out the recruiting force's high-profile position, which could play a role in influencing perceptions about the military: "We are the face of the Navy to the general U.S. population. I have no tolerance for that kind of breach of trust. We need families, communities, counselors, teachers to trust us and they deserve that level of trust . . . We follow policy to the law, and the law to the policy."

The Air Force aims to assure recruits that "the Air Force is completely focused on their safety." The Inspire, Deter, Detect, and Hold Accountable (IV2A) program is intended to introduce recruits to professional conduct and "what it means to be respectable in the Air Force." At different points in the recruiting process (e.g., at the recruiting station, before leaving for basic training), recruits are reminded of professional relationships and professional conduct, reiterating what is and is not acceptable. Just after arriving at basic training, recruits are asked about their recruiting experience to see if anything inappropriate occurred to them during the process.

Best Practices and Lessons Learned

We asked the senior leaders about what they considered to be successful recruiting practices and lessons learned. The Marine Corps commander stated his service's general approach as emphasizing service rather than a particular job: "Part of the sales process is first we sell the Marines, then we talk about what MOS you are interested in, we don't direct anyone into a particular field." The Marine Corps also "invests its best" in recruiting, selecting the top 10 percent of colonels and top 4 percent of majors for recruiting assignments and conducting multiple screenings of potential recruiters. Regarding its approach to recruiting women, the Marine Corps recruits women and men similarly, including equivalent methods and regulations. This approach reflects the Marine Corps' belief that a best practice is "inclusively recruiting females the same as males":

> That's a common refrain that we hear . . . they want to be treated the same. JAMRS interviews new applicants and they usually give it as a common refrain: not singled out. The Marine Corps talks about being inclusively recruited in the same matter. We find that in our daily practices to resonate fully, our most successful stations for recruiting females that's part of what they share is a common refrain . . . also inclusively recruiting females certainly is a best practice.

This approach represents a shift from two years ago, when the Marine Corps took different approaches to recruiting men and women. "Inclusive" recruiting has led to "encouraging results" in increased female recruitment. Also, tracking and "creating separate categories for female quality" and "missioning for a specific number of females" provided visibility of diversity that helped minimize potential disincentives for recruiters to spend the extra time to recruit women. In an effort to recruit inclusively, the Marine Corps has taken multiple paths, such as creating videos about what it is like to be a Marine, featuring women (e.g., helicopter pilot, aviation supply officer, Yale-educated lawyer) to allow them to "envision their self in that position."

The Marine Corps also tries to standardize training provided to recruits, viewing DEP training as an important opportunity to provide women with similar training to men, as well as leadership opportunities. Female-only DEP meetings are held to bring together female applicants and recruits from a single recruiting station or from several substations. These meetings provide women opportunities to "trade questions and concerns" and to trade social media contact information to form groups and eventually view themselves "not one of very few, but one of more and more." Female drill instructors or other female Marines in recruiting stations also help provide mentorship and answer questions. Another successful recruiting practice for the Marine Corps has been to specifically pursue potentially qualified applicants. This typically involves going to schools to attract "high-performing students and athletes and doing the work necessary to convince them to be U.S. Marines . . . rather than relying on referrals, women in the DEP, [recruiting] office traffic, etc." The Marine Corps commander also mentioned a recent effort to recruit women using a direct mailing campaign, which resulted in more responses than anticipated. Finally, he advised against directing or mandating people into specific jobs: "If we were in a position where we had to start directing, we would lose easily one-third into combat roles if we started directing women into combat roles."

The Navy mentioned two general approaches involving outreach to women who might be interested in joining. The first appears to be a longer-term approach of inspiring young women to consider science, technology, engineering, and math (STEM) careers, to "ensconce ourselves in the broader market" through engineering affinity groups and professional organizations (e.g., Society of Women Engineers). In addition, the Navy is seeking to engage elementary or middle schools to provide girls with hands-on experience in science fairs, underwater robotics, and other types of extracurricular STEM activity. The second approach to outreach is to ensure that advertising reflects the desired workforce diversity by, for instance, depicting "women in leadership series of fleet officers telling their stories." In the Navy recruiting leader's view, "no one tells our story better than our ambassadors who are living the dream."

The Air Force commander also mentioned the importance of community outreach, emphasizing the value of "face time" when recruiters were able to relate to people in the community. This could involve looking for specific events (e.g., women in aviation forums) where attendees could to relate to Air Force careers and potentially become interested in them. The Air Force commander also suggested the importance of considering retention alongside recruiting—for instance, that family-friendly policies should positively influence both potential recruits and their families. Accordingly, the Air Force has initiatives designed to retain women; for example, the Secretary of the Air Force announced 18 weeks of paid maternity leave.[1] The Air Force also offers childcare and a way to temporarily leave service for two or three years without incurring a negative impact on one's career.

How Best Practices Are Shared Across Recruiting Organizations

In addition to describing individual best practices, the senior leaders we interviewed described ways in which lessons learned were shared across the recruiting services. The Marine Corps, for instance, undertakes a structured process to share recruiting practices that appear to have had the greatest success:

> [We] just completed annual training . . . recruiting command . . . plus the sergeants, majors, plus my staff, etc. . . . We break down into separate working groups . . . Some of it is best practices from those recruiting stations that have shown the greatest success in low recruit training attrition and high quality numbers . . . And so, we asked those commanders to sit down as a group . . . trade best practices and provide the brief back to the entire audience in a different symposium.

The Navy's approach, "value oriented recruiting," seeks to incorporate lessons learned from marketing and advertising research about the recruiting market into its recruiting practices:

> We continue to be active in that regard . . . We try to understand where parts of the market are a little more open. We learn from our team, they our recruiters understand the approach, we call it value oriented recruiting, it's our sales and marketing campaign, best inform and influence, we are looking to inspire them and ultimately hire them. Some of it is based on geographic location, access to the fleet . . . We are constantly looking at better ways to do that.

[1] An OUSD/P&R policy, which Defense Secretary Ash Carter announced on January 28, 2016, would cut parental leave to 12 weeks.

Ways to Improve Ability to Recruit Qualified Youth

Overall, the services' recruiting leaders believe that recruiting qualified people to join the military will become increasingly difficult, expressing concerns about general recruiting trends and the resulting impact on their ability to recruit qualified individuals. The Army commander suggested that insufficient recruitment could become a "national security issue" if "we cannot recruit the caliber of people we need to sustain the all-volunteer force," and emphasized "find[ing] a way to really impress upon the political leadership the importance of getting the number higher than it is right now."

These leaders offered various suggestions for improving their ability to recruit, which fell into two broad themes: increasing the pool of qualified and youth, and increasing recruiting resources. It is worth noting that these themes are relevant for recruiting men as well as women, and they were discussed as such during our interviews with leadership.

Increase the Qualified and Motivated Pool of Youth

On the demand side, the recruiting leaders noted that requirements for both skills (e.g., STEM) and demographic diversity would likely continue to increase. The Navy commander emphasized the need for "our nation's finest STEM experts," for example, for jobs involving nuclear weapons in submarines. The leaders also pointed to multiple factors that affect the supply of willing and qualified youth, citing downward trends in youth who met moral, cognitive, and physical qualifications; lower unemployment in the general economy; and fewer influencers with military experience to encourage military service. For instance, the Air Force commander noted that people without military influencers might be less likely to view the military as a suitable career opportunity.

> The number of influencers that influence people to join the military are dwindling . . . So many, many people just don't understand the opportunities, and many people just don't understand the opportunities that exist and specifically for females.

The Army commander echoed the idea that youth have little awareness about the realities of military service.

> The youth of today, despite the fact of 14 years of a protracted land campaign, will stop us and thank us for our service. They really have no idea what service they are thanking us for. Other than we are protecting the homeland, they don't know what it means.

To raise awareness among and then attract qualified youth to the military, these leaders advocated for more outreach and engagement. According to the Air Force commander, "It's not about selection or a hiring, it's about exposure—incentivizing people to come into the Air Force based on what they want from us and what we can offer them." The Navy commander recommended considering marketing and advertising in conjunction with other options, such as recruiting incentives:

> There's the market, the requirements, and we are in a resource-constrained environment. You see the DoD top line and that affects some choices . . . We have to look at manpower, marketing, advertising, and how we have to look at things like enlistment bonuses, and those are always on the table, it's up to me to make sure we are getting a return on our

> investment from everything we do . . . when you put the levers together, it portends that we are going to be more challenged in the future.

According to recruiting leadership, this outreach and engagement should seek to increase the number of qualified individuals and to increase information about the military and awareness of it as a viable career option among qualified individuals. On the potential impact of doing this, the Army commander stressed the value of finding a way to increase the pool of qualified youth:

> One thing that would really help is if more men and women were actually qualified to join the Army . . . Only three in ten are actually able to meet the cognitive, physical, and moral component in order to actually join the Army. When you ask me, what could make your job easier? Well, if you can increase the number of qualified military applicants, in the pool, and you could raise that number to four in ten that are actually qualified, that would be huge.

The Navy commander emphasized the potential impact of demographic diversity for increasing broad awareness of the military:

> We—at least at DoD, the U.S. government—we need to make what we do in the service of our nation, attractive to everybody in the U.S. early so they can get excited about it . . . so they can be empowered and educated to make a bold step . . . and eventually it won't be such a bold step . . . It is just who we are . . . It is more representative of our country and the people who compose our country. That would be my general recommendation to make us be more effective by helping us in getting our story out there . . . making sure people understand what it is that we are here to do.

The service leaders also suggested other ways to increase awareness and propensity, such as opportunities for internships to excite youth about the possibility of the military at an early age, which could make them more likely to join later on and potentially ease parents' anxieties. Another suggestion was a "national campaign call to service" that would buttress the services' individual marketing and advertising with a campaign focused more broadly on "general service to military." Finally, the leaders suggested increasing access to schools to "debunk myths" about the military, particularly in private schools and areas of the country with fewer influencers. The recruiting leaders believed that limited recruiter access had the effect of constraining "[youths'] ability to make an informed decision." Increased access would not only provide youth with information about the realities of military life, but could inspire and engage youth to consider military careers as more than just a job and as a potential "transformative experience."

Increase Resources for Advertising and Outreach and Ease Burden on Recruiters

Senior leaders highlighted increasing recruiting resources as an action that could improve recruiting in multiple ways and allow them to implement targeted or innovative actions for which they did not have sufficient resources. First, increased resources for advertising and marketing were seen as especially important to counteract trends of decreasing influencers that can provide firsthand knowledge about the military. According to the Air Force commander, "a properly resourced campaign from the perspective of a female serving in our ranks" and "campaigns to break down the myths" are needed. Similarly, the Army commander emphasized "highlight[ing] the available opportunities to women via marketing/advertising efforts. We want to increase the number of women making the decision to better represent both the Army and the society."

Both the Air Force and Army commanders stated that resources for targeted outreach would help reach specific populations, including women. For instance, the Army commander mentioned a significant Army-wide marketing effort, Enterprise Army Branding, that, in his view, should be complemented with local advertising efforts:

> You don't have to be a rocket scientist to figure out that, depending on what part of the country you are at recruiting young men and women, they are going to want examples of people who have joined from their area that look like them, that have actually made that decision. I don't know that the national campaign is really going to do that.

The Air Force commander listed a number of targeted outreach actions that they had been unable to take, due to lack of resources:

> [We could reach out to] female guidance counselors, female educators . . . but we haven't had money to do an educator tour in four or five years . . . Those are the types of things I can target . . . What we don't have is the luxury of targeting a specific group, it's not just limited to females . . . We can't go [on] Spanish radio stations, not because we don't want to, but because we don't have any money. If you stop under-resourcing us, [provide] the money to do a proper campaign at addressing women's concerns . . . we could really do some innovative things . . . If we just had a little bit of money, we could go to female colleges, to female private schools, to get those influencers and we could bring them down here, take them to the Riverwalk, then they could immediately fall in love.

More resources could also increase the number of recruiters to generate leads and work with potential recruits and influencers. Air Force leadership referred to a "funnel effect" in which people are weeded out and disqualified, but more recruiters in the field could find more people and thus expand the potential applicant pool:

> Give us more recruiters. I know that sounds flippant; you have to pay for it. At the end of the day, if you want a bigger pool of applicants you have to pay for it. There is an art to this . . . Great recruiters know they aren't better than anyone else . . . They know the art, but there is also a science to it . . . They get 36 percent of their leads—out of 100, they will get 36 in . . . If you want to increase the number of women, I need to increase the number of leads. How do you do that? Put a little more money into recruiting . . . It really becomes a math thing.

The Army commander noted that male recruiters across the organization have told leadership that more female recruiters were needed. Female recruiters also told leadership that female recruiters were more successful than male recruiters in recruiting women. Finding these statements "compelling," Army leadership examined gender representation in the recruiting force. Because the recruiting force is 8 to 9 percent women, compared with 15 percent women across the Army, recruiting leadership communicated the need for more female recruiters to U.S. Army Training and Doctrine Command and asked to increase the number of female recruiters by 1 percent each year to reach the level of overall representation in the Army. While the Army commander acknowledged the difficulty in competing for women to be recruiters, he underscored the importance of having visible women during the recruiting process:

> When you talk about recruiters and the screening required, that small percentage of women that the Army has, we are all vying for that cut . . . I want them to recruit. We also need them to be drill sergeants and advanced individual training; we also need them in the schoolhouse. The challenge is how do you divide them up between the groups? What I've asked for, I understand there is fierce competition . . . and they can't be by themselves. So [recruits] are met with and received so they can identify with someone in the formation. We need noncommissioned officers.

Senior leaders also suggested that increased recruiting resources could serve to mitigate recruiter burden and challenges they faced. According to the Marine Corps commander, because more time is needed to contract women than for men, the Marine Corps Commandant's decision to increase female percentage above 10 percent end strength by 2021 would increase responsibilities and time burden for recruiters. The Army commander suggested that increased recruiting resources could also boost recruiter morale if used to restore special duty assignment pay for recruiters. Maintaining Army recruiter morale had been a challenge because of the increased scrutiny of social media and the "small world we live in," as well as because (unlike other services) Army recruiters' special duty assignment pay was cut, even though the Army bore the largest recruiting mission.

Key Findings

- Recruiters in our focus groups report disincentives and barriers to recruiting women. For example, leadership and recruiters also cited that women were harder to recruit and more likely to be lost in the DEP. Recruiters also noted that men have a hard time recruiting women because of concerns about perceptions of inappropriate relationships.
- Recruiters and recruits in our focus groups report dissatisfaction with what they view as burdensome administrative requirements.
- Commanders of the recruiting services report concern over resources available to them in the current recruiting environment, and suggest increasing recruiting resources.
- Recruiters, recruits, and leadership all agree that increased advertising targeting women and greater access to female military role models would be beneficial.

CHAPTER SIX

Limitations, Key Findings, and Recommendations

As a reminder, OSD asked us to explore how the opening of combat jobs to women might affect recruiting and identify ways to mitigate any potential negative impacts. It also asked for suggestions for ways to increase the recruitment of women in general, as women are still significantly underrepresented in the force as a whole.

In response to how opening combat jobs to women might affect recruiting, our results suggest that it is not likely to cause major recruiting issues going forward. Based on the results of the interviews and focus groups, we did not see signs that opening combat jobs to women would have a major chilling effect on people's willingness to join. Many of our male participants expressed that the policy change did not factor into their decision to join at all. And many women expressed the opposite sentiment: that women would even be more willing to apply because of the greater sense of equality that the policy change would afford them. Of course, as discussed below, our participants only included people who had already volunteered for service, not those who decided against it. Nevertheless, if a large chilling effect on willingness to join were occurring, we would expect to hear many more negative sentiments about the policy than we did.

In response to the second request by OSD (suggestions for ways to increase recruitment of women), the results of the focus groups suggest several strategies. Those are discussed below. However, before we discuss the recommendations, we discuss some of the limitations for the work and recap the major findings.

Limitations

What we heard in the focus groups and interviews was broadly consistent with other research, including JAMRS research findings. Nevertheless, the focus groups and interviews on which we have based these findings have some important limitations. The first limitation involves potential selection bias. Our focus groups with recent recruits were limited to people who had made the decision to join the military, and thus do not represent those who were unsure about or had decided against joining the military. Furthermore, the focus group participants were not randomly selected, and therefore did not necessarily constitute a representative sample of those who had joined the military. For instance, recruits had been in the DEP (i.e., they had agreed to join military service but were waiting to ship out for training) for different lengths of time. During this time, their perceptions may have been altered by exposure to military culture, or they could have misremembered details about recruiting experience if it had taken place much earlier. An uneven participant distribution (e.g., more men than women, more enlistees than officers) may also limit the generalizability of our findings for particular groups.

Another limitation involves the interpersonal interaction inherent in either face-to-face or group settings, which may have introduced response biases such as social desirability (i.e., participants may have only expressed opinions they thought were acceptable to others in the group). We sought to address potential response bias, such as minimizing discomfort addressing sensitive issues (e.g., concerns about sexual harassment or assault) by allowing participants to raise them organically in discussion and by matching researcher-participant gender when possible. In addition, after each focus group, we also directly asked participants whether they felt comfortable answering our questions, and participants wholeheartedly responded in the affirmative. Although the women said that they felt comfortable talking about these issues in the group, it is still possible that they may not have been forthright in their responses on topics such as sexual assault/harassment.

It is also important to note that in our findings we discuss instances in which at least a few focus groups raised a given comment. However, failure of other focus groups to mention a given comment or failure for the comment to come up in most of the focus groups does not necessarily mean that others disagree with it. For example, when we report that 93 percent of the female focus groups report viewing women in the military positively, this does not mean that the remaining 7 percent do not view women in the military positively, but rather that they simply did not respond with a positive statement, such as "Women in the military are great," in response to our question: What do you think about women serving in the military?

We also want to remind readers that the percentages reported throughout the report refer to the percentage of groups in which a comment was mentioned, not the percentage of respondents who mentioned it. As a result, even comments that occurred in a majority of the groups may not be comments about which participants tend to agree. For example, in 79 and 80 percent of the female and male focus groups, respectively, someone expressed a desire to go into combat; however, this cannot be interpreted to mean that the percentage of women who would be willing to go into combat is the same as the percentage of men willing, but rather that there is sufficient interest by some women that it should not be disregarded. Readers are also cautioned that, because these are counts of spontaneous comments, care should be taken to not interpret the statistics imply the converse of a statement. For example, while 13 percent of male focus groups had someone who explicitly stated that they would go into combat if called upon, it does not mean that participants in the remaining 87 percent of focus groups would not be willing to go into combat if called upon. (For more on this, refer to Chapter Two.)

Lastly, our sample sizes limit some of our conclusions and analyses. First, it is not feasible with such small sample sizes to do statistical tests of the differences between services or regions of the country. Although we could not do those tests, we can say that our general impression of the discussions was that the comments were similar regardless of location. With respect to service differences, the discussions were different in some predictable ways but not in ways that were meaningful for the findings in the study. That is, the groups expressed pride in their own service and differences in the service cultures were apparent (Marines acted like Marines, airmen acted like airmen, etc.). However, when it came to talking about the issues of women in combat, responses were remarkably similar across services. The Army and Marine Corps personnel talked more about life in combat settings and the potential for them to be asked to go into combat; however, like the participants in the Air Force and Navy, they tended to speak positively about women in the military and about opening up combat jobs to women who could meet the standards. Second, due to scheduling difficulties, we had fewer Army focus groups than for the other services. As a result, their views are not equally represented in the overall findings, even though they are the service with the largest number of jobs that will be affected by the combat policy change. Nevertheless, as noted above, we did not notice any meaningful differences in the types of responses given by the Army participants that might warrant concern. Third, our four officer focus groups represent views from only two services (one group was from the Air Force and three were from the Marine Corps), again because of scheduling difficulties. As a result, we cannot know whether views from the other services would be likely to be different.

Overall Findings

There were many interesting findings from the focus groups that could be useful for informing recruiting approaches and even changes to recruiting policies. However, the following five findings are particularly noteworthy:

- Many female recruits prefer female recruiters and are less concerned about sexual harassment and assault than their influencers.
- Many male recruits reported that their decision to was not affected by the policy change and report feeling that women should be allowed into combat if they can meet the same standards as men.
- Many recruiters are also not concerned about the policy change, but report disincentives and barriers to recruiting women.
- Many recruiters and recruits report dissatisfaction with what they view as burdensome administrative requirements.
- Commanders of the recruiting services report a strong desire to recruit more women through targeted outreach and increased advertising but expressed concern that the resources available to them were insufficient to accomplish such targeted efforts.

Recommendations

Based on these findings, in order to recruit more women and to improve recruiting overall, we recommend the following.

Increase the Proportion of Recruiters Who Are Women and Create Programs and Strategically Place Them to Maximize Their Impact

Many of our participants (recruiters and recruits alike) believe that greater female presence among recruiters is critical to attracting more women. Recruits believed that the increased visibility of women in uniform at recruiting events would help break down stereotypes that the military is not a career choice for women. By seeing women in uniform in person, they may be better able to envision themselves in that role. In addition, access to women recruiters during the recruiting process (even if their recruiter is male) was another way that recruits and recruiters believed that the military could attract more women. Female recruiters have firsthand experiences to share with recruits, which was greatly appreciated by many of those who participated in our female focus groups. Many female recruits also expressed feeling more comfortable with key aspects of the military and the enlistment process when there was a female available to answer questions that might be gender-specific or where they believe the perspectives of women might differ from that of men.

In light of these comments, we suggest not only increasing the numbers of female recruiters, but also strategically using them to make sure they have the desired impact. That includes doing the following:

- **Dispersing female recruiters across recruiting stations to maximize coverage.** Because the overall proportion of women in the services is low, the proportion of recruiters who are female is also low. However, this lack of visibility may be perpetuating the problem. For that reason, we recommend not only boosting the numbers of female recruiters but also taking care to spread them across all recruiting stations to maximize their impact.
- **Ensuring female recruiters are highly visible at recruiting events.** If female recruiters are made visible and even showcased at public recruiting events (i.e., made visible outside of the recruiting station), it may help generate greater interest among women who are not already inclined to military service. One participant recalled not seeing any women in uniform at her high school military recruiting event (the representatives from all four services were male), which discouraged her from volunteering. To reduce burden on female recruiters (as their numbers are naturally fewer than that of the men), the services could team up and trade off on providing a uniformed woman for such events.
- **Creating programs to make sure all female recruits and potential recruits have access to female mentors.** Recruits could be assigned to a recruiter of either gender (regardless of their own gender), but all female recruits should also be given direct one-on-one access to at least one specially designated local female recruiter whose job it is to share about her experience serving as a woman and answer questions about issues that female recruits might feel uncomfortable raising with male recruiters. That designated recruiter's job would be to regularly and continuously reach out to each female recruit (and potential recruit, where possible) and hold periodic discussions with them as needed.
- **Organizing regular (e.g., monthly) group events so all female recruits have a chance to have face-to-face contact with female recruiters.** Recruiting offices could hold group events where all potential and current female recruits meet with a designated female recruiter as well as other available female military servicemembers. This could allow them to hear questions from other female recruits, develop rapport with the female recruiters, and get greater exposure to female role models. We suggest inviting guests who represent a range of female perspectives, including women who just completed basic training, women who have served for many years, and women with different types of jobs.

Increase Outreach Targeted Towards Women

Participants believed that increased exposure to women in the military by the public at large could help generate interest among women who would otherwise never have considered joining. They explained that many in the public hold stereotypes that are based on Hollywood's depiction of the military—conjuring up images of combat-related activities and little else. People who are uninterested in combat-type jobs then cannot envision themselves pursuing a career in the military.

Our participants noted that this is a misperception that both men and women in the public hold; they therefore recommended eliminating this stereotype to increase recruitment of both groups. Nevertheless, they believed that the stereotype might be a bigger obstacle or more widespread issue among women. Our participants believed one of the best ways to change this stereotype was through advertising depicting men and women engaging in a wide range of military jobs, especially those that defy the combat-heavy stereotype.

In addition, recruits and recruiters described how many military jobs that are not directly tied to combat (e.g., equipment maintenance and engineering-type jobs) are still perceived as male-dominated and therefore not something women are naturally drawn to. In spite of this, women serve and have very successful military careers in these jobs. Our participants suggested advertising that shows women serving in those jobs, excelling at them, and really enjoying the work to help defy that stereotype as well.

In addition, as noted above, participants strongly suggested that involving more women in recruiting events would be another good way to help generate interest in serving among women who may not have previously considered the idea. Increasing the presence of women in service at recruiting events may be effective at generating interest among women who had not previously considered serving, but recruiting activities and events targeted specifically towards women should also be explored. For example, recruiters could arrange activities with women's sports teams or hold events to teach high school students about opportunities for women the military.

The goals behind targeted advertising and targeted recruiting activities would be to encourage more women to think things like: "Wow, that woman has a really exciting job," "If she can do that job, maybe I could too," and "She seems happy working in the military, maybe I would be too," and ultimately to generate interest among a larger population of women than have been interested in the past. However, additional research should follow up to evaluate the effectiveness of such targeted advertising and recruiting efforts at sparking interest among new populations of women.

In our discussions with recruiting leadership, they expressed a strong desire to engage in the types of targeted recruiting activities described above, but noted that to do so would require reallocating resources in their already tight recruiting budgets. Therefore, if recruiting more women is an important OSD goal, the services would benefit from OSD assistance in securing more funding for such activities. Alternatively, OSD could consider pursuing those activities on behalf of the services. For example, OSD could (with service input and assistance) create their own advertising and education campaigns targeted towards women.

To sum up, we recommend the following:

- creating additional advertising and promotional materials highlighting the variety of roles that women fill in the military services and countering stereotypes and misperceptions about military service
- taking advantage of recruiting practices that can be focused on women (e.g., women-only events at schools)
- conducting follow-up studies to determine the effectiveness of targeted advertising and recruiting events.

Reduce Administrative Burdens on Recruiters and Recruits

Lastly, many of our participants suggested that reducing administrative burdens would help with recruiting. Many recruiters lamented the fact that they lose some interested recruits during the recruiting process, and they specifically noted that women are consistently more likely to be lost during the recruiting process than men. Some recruits may find other employment options while they are waiting to be processed or shipped off to training; others may have second thoughts as a result of discussions with family and friends. Given this, some of our recruiter participants believe that more recruits of both genders, but especially female recruits, would complete the process if the delays between expressing interest and being sent off to training could be reduced. They therefore suggested that reducing and streamlining administrative burdens would be a good solution. Some recruits echoed the complaint, noting that the process is long and requires so many steps that it is easy to see why some people fail to follow through on the entire application process.

In addition, recruiters noted that they themselves are burdened with various paperwork and other administrative requirements (detailed timekeeping was one example provided by our participants). This takes time away from talking to recruits, attending recruiting events, and engaging in other recruiting activities. Reducing the administrative burdens on recruiters would therefore free up time for the recruiters to execute their mission.

We therefore suggest pursuing the following:

- revising requirements on recruiters, such as detailed timekeeping, to reduce the time taken away from recruiting activities
- making better use of technology, such as channeling information from one form to others so that the same information does not have to be entered multiple times
- streamlining the recruiting process to shorten the time from initial contact to ship date.

Caveats to Our Recommendations

Although our recommendations follow directly from our focus group findings, we offer a few important caveats that should be considered before any new recruiting policies are implemented.

Limitations of the Study Need to Be Considered

Do we know these recommendations will lead to measurably better results in recruiting women? The short answer is: no. At the start of this chapter, we discussed several important methodological limitations to our research study. Our recommendations need to be weighed in the context of those limitations.

Most notably, the focus group approach and focus group population both prevent us from being able to say definitively whether or not our recommendations would have the desired effect. Our recommendations are based on opinions, attitudes, and speculation voiced during focus groups and interviews. It is very possible that opinion, attitudes, and speculation may not have any validity when it comes to identifying effective strategies for recruiting women. However, in the absence of any other information, we believe it is a starting point for ideas.

In addition, we noted at the outset of this study that we could not access the ideal population of interest: female youth who are not yet interested in serving.[1] Instead, our recommendations come from views expressed by people who have already made the decision to join the military and from military personnel (recruiters and recruiting leadership) who are already steeped in the military culture. We therefore fully acknowledge that the participant views that informed our recommendations may be distinctly different from those who chose not to join. Our recommendations might have been different had we interviewed those who chose *not* to join.

However, as noted above, in the absence of any other information, we believe the views of our sample of participants (recent recruits, recruiters, and recruiting leadership) are still useful for generating ideas for improving the recruitment of women. Now that a set of ideas for changes to recruiting practices have been identified, a next step towards a more definitive answer would be to implement some of the recommendations and test out their effectiveness.

Costs and Tradeoffs Need to Be Considered

It is also important to note that the recommendations we offered above are not cost free.

Some of the costs come in the form of additional resources. For example there are added costs associated with creating separate recruiting materials, holding special events, and rolling out advertising specifically designed to target women. In addition, it is clear from our interviews with recruiters and leadership that more time and effort are needed to recruit women than men, and that women have a higher attrition rate from the DEP. Both are key observations that bear directly on the expected return to additional investments in recruiting women. While the additional resources may increase the number of women recruited, the return on these investments may not be as high (in terms of number of additional bodies recruited and retained) as the return on other recruiting endeavors.

There are also other costs that come in the form of tradeoffs or unintended consequences. For example, if more women are placed in recruiting duties, there will be fewer women out performing the mission. This could make women even more of a minority in some situations, which could perpetuate stereotypes and perceptions that there are very few women in certain jobs. And if women are more likely than men to be sent to recruiting duties or asked to stay there longer than their male counterparts, it may ultimately hinder their career progression because they will have to spend more time away from their core job. This could hurt women as a whole in the services in the long run, even if it may help with recruiting of new women. If such an effort is made to divert more women to the recruiting cause, then efforts should be made to prevent negative effects on women's career progression.

In addition (although perhaps an obvious point), an increase in the proportion of female new recruits necessarily means that there would have to be a concomitant decrease in the proportion of male recruits. It is worth noting that is unlikely to be seen by OSD and the services as a negative, considering their stated goal to increase representation of women in the services; however, it is a tradeoff, and is therefore is included here.

---

[1] As noted previously, the period of performance on this project was not long enough to allow for us to apply for OMB clearance (an approval process that takes a minimum of six months), which is required when federal funds are used to collect data on members of the public. Instead, with the support of our sponsor, we decided that the recent recruit population would have to serve as our best available proxy for the civilian youth population, with the full recognition that recent recruits already have a propensity for military service since they joined the service.

These are just a few examples of the many costs, tradeoffs, and other potential unintended consequences that need to be considered and weighed in decisions about how to proceed. These issues, costs, and tradeoffs, however, are not insurmountable. Given that OSD and the services have expressed a strong interest in finding ways to recruit more women, the suggestions offered here are still worthy of consideration, assuming that the tradeoffs discussed above are ones that the services are willing to accept. Nevertheless, closely monitoring the success of such efforts would be wise, to ensure that the obvious tradeoffs and costs associated with them are truly justified. In cases where full implementation would be expensive, pilot testing could be an important first step. Such pilot testing would allow for an initial assessment of not only the impact of a recommended change, but also an exploration of the potential costs and unintended consequences that might result.

Closing Thoughts

As we usher in a new era of equality for women in the military—one in which anyone who can demonstrate the abilities necessary to do the job can serve in that job—the number of jobs available to women will increase dramatically. As a result, women in uniform will likely begin to be increasingly visible in jobs across the services (especially in the Army and Marine Corps, where the majority of the jobs were previously closed). These increased opportunities offer new avenues for women to have a successful military career and could be an important driver for generating interest among women who may not have previously considered serving. This policy change therefore brings with it new chances to grow the representation of women in the service beyond the levels of the past.

This study was designed to provide initial suggestions for how the services could take steps to generate such new interest. Overall, our results suggest that more certainly could be done to target women who have not previously expressed interest; however, as noted above, such efforts come with added costs that need to be considered. Nevertheless, we offer a number of initial suggestions for actions that could be pursued to help recruit more female youth. Ultimately, how successful those efforts would be at increasing representation of women in the services remains to be seen. That question can best be answered by implementing the suggestions discussed here and following up with additional research on their effectiveness. As such, this work is just a first step towards finding the policies that are most effective at increasing representation of women in the services. More work will undoubtedly be needed.

APPENDIX A

Focus Group and Interview Questions

Focus Group Questions for Recent Military Recruits

[*Administer consent*]

Icebreaker

Tell me a little about your background. Where are you from originally?

Thoughts About the Military and Sources of Information

When did you start thinking about joining the military?

What were the most **appealing** things about joining the military? Did you have any **concerns** about joining the military? If so, what were they?

How did you first come into contact with a recruiter? (phone call, school visit, recruiting office, etc.)

- What has the recruiter done or told you to make the military more/less appealing?
- What incentives, if any, were offered to you during the recruitment process? (incentive pays, delayed entry program, etc.?) Did these incentives help to sway your decision to join or to select a specific rate/MOS?

Where do you normally find out about what is happening locally, nationally, and in the world?

- Newspapers? Print? Online?
- Television or radio news shows?
- Internet news sources?
- Facebook?
- Twitter?

From which of these sources did you learn about the military?

Who did you talk with when you were deciding whether to join the military (parents, teachers, friends?)

- Who was most influential in your decision?
- What were their reasons for supporting/not supporting your decision to join?

What were the most important factors in your decision to apply to the military? Is there anything that would have made it even easier for you to decide?

[*FEMALE ONLY*] Did you talk to other women specifically to get their perspective on serving in the military? Who?

[*FEMALE ONLY*] Do you have female friends who decided not to join the military? Why not?

Gender-Related Questions

Now we would like to ask you a few questions related to gender.

In general, what do you think about women serving in the military?

Did the role of women in the military factor into your decision to join at all?

[MALES AND FEMALES] Do you know any women who have served in the military? Have you talked with them about their military experience? If so, how did that impact your decision?

Was your recruiter a woman or a man? *For those with a male recruiter*: If the recruiter was a woman, would it have affected your perception of the military? If so, how? For those with a female recruiter, did that change your perception of the military at all?

Did you, or do you now know that women are no longer banned from serving in combat?

- Did it affect your decision to join? (*if known beforehand*) Would this have affected your decision to join? (*if not known beforehand*)
- What do you think about women serving in combat roles?
- Do you have any interest in serving in a combat role? Why or why not?
- Do you think this repeal of the ban on women in combat will affect your career in the military? How?
- [*FEMALE ONLY*] Do you have any concerns about serving in a majority-male organization? Why or why not?

Closing Questions

What changes should be made to support recruitment of women into the armed services?

What do you think would make the military more appealing to your friends who might not have considered applying? (*for women, ask about female friends specifically*)

[*Ask opposite gender researcher to leave.*] How comfortable were you answering these questions in with a man/woman in the room. Is there anything you would like to say now that you didn't feel comfortable talk about with them in the room?

Any other questions or thoughts?

Interview Questions for Military Recruiters

[*Administer consent*]

General Background Questions (10 minutes)

- How long have you been in this post as a recruiter?
- How were you assigned this job? Did you request it?
- Do you have any previous experience with recruiting before this assignment? (When, where?)
- Have you received recruitment training? What info or directions are you given?

Topic: What do recruiters do to recruit? (5 minutes)

Could you tell us a little bit about how you find recruits and bring them in?

Do you have any targets that you need to meet? (skills, diversity, gender, specific rates, etc.)

Do you find that it is easier/harder to recruit for certain jobs or from certain demographics?

Are your recruits able to select their MOS upon entry or are they assigned based on need? Does this vary by the type of recruit?

Topic: What are recruiting best practices? (10 minutes)

Are there any well-established best-practices for recruiting?

- What sort of recruiting tools do you have at your disposal? (incentive pays, delayed entry program, etc.?)
- What is the best way to reach out to and identify new recruits? (Any "tricks of the trade")
- Do you have any resources for "best practices" that were given to you by previous recruiters or during training?

Topic: Are there different approaches to recruiting men and women? Should there be? Do recruiters have incentives or disincentives for recruiting women? (15 minutes)

Do you try to recruit women? Why or why not? What about other recruiters?

Are there incentives/disincentives for recruiting women?

How do you go about recruiting women?

- Do you find that women are more receptive to different recruiting approaches?
- What approach has been most successful for you in recruiting women?

What career fields/MOS do you find that women are more interested in? How about men?

About what percentage of your new recruits are female? About what percentage of the women that you *try* to recruit end up signing up?

Topic: How informed are recruits? What are their information sources? (5 minutes)

Do you find that potential recruits are generally well informed about military service and the jobs available to them? Are there differences in how well informed women are vs. men?

Where do male/female recruits typically get information from about the military?

Topic: Who are the key influencers for women joining the military? (10 minutes)

Do you find that there are outside influencers (parents, friends, teachers) that affect women's decisions to enter the military?

- What are the concerns of these outside influences?
- How do you address those concerns?

Topic: What concerns do women express about entering the military? (5 minutes)

What kind of concerns or reservations do women express about entering the military? About entering into combat roles?

- Are these concerns the same/different than the concerns you see from male recruits? How do you address these concerns?

Topic: Have recruiting policies/behaviors changed in response to combat roles being opened? What about in response to "hot topics" (i.e., sexual harassment or assault)? (10 minutes)

What do you know about the repeal of the exclusion of women from combat roles?

- Will this apply to the positions you recruit for? Which ones?
- Has this changed/will this change your approaches to recruiting?

Are your potential recruits aware of this change?

- Has it affected their perceptions of the military?
- Has it affected your ability to recruit women or men?

Do you see any interest from women in pursuing combat MOSs?

- Of the women who are interested in combat roles, do they have any specific attributes?

Do you find that women are concerned about sexual harassment/sexual assault in the military? How do you address these concerns?

Closing Questions

Do you have any suggestions for changes that can be made that could improve your ability to recruit women into the military or to improve the recruiting environment more generally?

Interview Questions for Recruiting Leadership

[*Administer consent*]

Topic: What do they currently do to recruit women? What are the obstacles?

Do you have general recruiting goals/ targets for women in your branch of the service?

- How do you track it?
- Do you incentivize it?
- Are you generally reaching these targets?
- Do these targets vary by job type/MOS/rating?

What are major obstacles for recruiting women?

- How does this differ from recruiting men?

Topic: What are some recruiting best practices?

Do you have any best practices or lessons learned from your top recruiters?

Are these the same or different for recruiting men versus recruiting women? Or for male versus female recruiters?

Do you have any suggestions for changes that can be made that could improve the recruitment of women into the military or to improve the recruiting environment more generally?

Topic: Have/will recruiting policies/behaviors changed in response to combat roles being opened? What about in response to "hot topics" (i.e. sexual harassment or assault)?

How will the opening of combat roles for women affect recruiting in your branch of the service?

- Do you foresee any challenges in recruiting women into combat roles?

- Do you foresee any new challenges in recruiting men when combat roles become open for women?

Do you plan on adjusting your recruiting strategies/goals/targets as combat roles become open for women?

- How will this be implemented? (recruiter training, new policies, advertising campaigns, etc.)
- What concerns, if any, do you have about the implementation?

Have there been any recruiting policy changes or guidance for recruiters in response to recent events? (i.e., high-profile sexual assault cases)

APPENDIX B

Themes from Focus Groups and Interviews

The tables in this appendix list the full set of themes we identified from the focus groups and interviews with enlisted recruits and recruiters (see Tables 2.1–2.3 for numbers of participants). This set of themes therefore includes the findings reported in the main body of this report, as well as additional responses that were mentioned but not frequently enough to warrant inclusion in the main findings. Responses in Tables B.1 through B.5 are grouped thematically and then sorted in descending order by percentage of female focus groups in which they were mentioned.

We identified these themes based on the original research questions and focus group protocol, adding additional themes that surfaced during the coding process (see Chapter Two for details of this methodology). After reconciling coding schemes (86 percent agreement), we finalized the lists of themes for the enlisted recruits and recruiters. For the few remaining coding disagreements after reconciliation, we used the more conservative (i.e., lower) estimate. For instance, if one coder coded a theme as mentioned in one focus group, but the other coder did not mark that theme in any focus groups, we report that theme conservatively—in other words, we would report that theme as being mentioned by zero percent of focus groups.

Because we spoke with relatively fewer officers and recruiting leadership, we did not conduct this coding, and therefore those themes are not reported here.

Table B.1
Perceptions, Attitudes, and Awareness: Themes from Enlisted Recruit Focus Groups

Theme	Female Focus Groups	Male Focus Groups
Women in the military		
Generally view women in the military as good/positive	93%	80%
Generally view women in the military as bad/negative	0%	7%
Women in combat roles		
Aware of policy change to open combat jobs to women before joining	79%	67%
Unaware of the policy change to open combat jobs to women	50%	53%
Mentioned something either neutral or positive about the policy change	93%	87%
Mentioned that women should be allowed in combat if they can pass the same tests and meet the same standards as men	21%	80%
Concern that standards should not be lowered	7%	40%
Concern with women in combat is that men would go help women first, regardless of the situation	7%	7%
Aware of policy change to open combat jobs to women only after joining	7%	0%
Concern with women in combat is that women won't be able to carry men if they need to	7%	0%
Desire to go to combat		
Would like to go into combat	79%	80%
Do not want to go into combat	43%	7%
Not interested in going into combat, but would go into combat if called upon	29%	13%
Sources of general news		
Television	86%	80%
Internet	64%	73%
Social media	64%	33%
Other people	21%	27%
Sources of military news		
Directly from the services (e.g., newsfeed, emails, website)	71%	60%
YouTube	29%	20%
Generally online	14%	27%
Social media (e.g., Facebook, Instagram, Twitter)	14%	7%
Perceptions about other services		
Perceive the Marines to be "the few, the proud," generally a superior service	29%	27%
Did not like that recruiter(s) from the other services ignored my initiative/attempts to apply	21%	0%
Perceive Air Force to have highest quality of life	7%	40%
When first considered joining the military		
Started thinking about joining the military in high school	100%	73%
Started thinking about joining the military when I was little	50%	73%
Started thinking about joining the military in the past year	50%	53%

Table B.2
Influences for Joining: Themes from Enlisted Recruit Focus Groups

Theme	Female Focus Groups	Male Focus Groups
Appeals of joining the military		
Education benefits	93%	80%
Opportunity to travel	71%	80%
Opportunity for self-improvement	71%	80%
Noneducation benefits associated with military service	64%	47%
Being independent	43%	13%
The sense of pride/honor/respect from serving	29%	60%
Military pay	29%	40%
Civilian opportunities after military service	29%	20%
Opportunity to serve country	0%	33%
Concerns about joining the military		
Being away from family and friends	36%	40%
Possibility of deployment/war	29%	27%
Physical training requirements/rules regarding weight	29%	20%
No concerns when joining because I knew what I was getting into	21%	47%
Possibility of injury/death	14%	33%
Not knowing where they would be stationed	7%	7%
Concerns about sexual harassment and assault		
No concerns about serving in a majority male organization	50%	0%
The risk of sexual harassment/assault in and out of the military seems about the same, so I'm not worried	21%	0%
Was not worried about sexual harassment/assault, but began to worry because it was brought up so many times during recruiting process	14%	0%
Was not worried about sexual harassment/assault	14%	0%
Was worried about sexual harassment/assault, but then learned about the buddy system that eased concerns	7%	0%
Was worried about sexual/assault harassment and assault	7%	0%
Most important influencers		
Parents were most important influencers	29%	27%
Did not consult with influencers and made the decision independently	21%	40%
Recruiters		
Gender of the recruiter did not matter	71%	73%
Having a female recruiter would have made it easier to join	57%	7%
Recruiters who could answer female-specific questions positively influenced decision to join	36%	0%
Recruiter was a positive influence for joining	14%	13%
Recruiter was a negative influence for joining	0%	0%
Family		
Parents were supportive	71%	67%
Family was supportive of one service over another	50%	27%
Did not inform parents of decision to join until after the decision was made	21%	0%

Table B.2—Continued

Theme	Female Focus Groups	Male Focus Groups
Friends		
Nonmilitary friends were not supportive of decision to join	64%	40%
Nonmilitary friends were supportive of decision to join	21%	20%
Family or friends with military service		
Current or previous military friends/family were supportive of decision to join	86%	73%
Current or previous military friends/family were not supportive	7%	27%
Influencers' reasons to support joining the military		
Greater independence (personal, financial, and otherwise)	7%	0%
Pay	7%	0%
Influencers' reasons to not support joining the military		
Concerns about injury	71%	47%
Concerns about sexual harassment/assault	50%	0%
Concerns about deployment	21%	0%
Women in the military and decision to join		
The role of women in the military did not factor into decision to join	43%	47%
The role of women in the military factored into decision to join	43%	0%
Did not believe the policy change to open combat jobs to women would impact their career	36%	53%
Policy change to open combat jobs to women had no impact on the decision to join	21%	73%
Reasons why friends did not join the military		
Too lazy to undergo the process	36%	20%
Could not qualify	29%	0%
Prefer to work or go to college first	7%	13%

Table B.3
Recruiting Policies and Strategies: Themes from Enlisted Recruit Focus Groups

Theme	Female Focus Groups	Male Focus Groups
Positive things recruiters did		
Was transparent and honest	86%	67%
Was available at all times	14%	7%
Facilitated female-only group sessions to answer female questions	36%	0%
Used personal experience as an example	14%	0%
Provided escort to MEPS	14%	0%
Negative things recruiter did		
Did not provide escort to MEPS	14%	0%
Pressured the recruit and seemed desperate	7%	0%
Nothing the recruiter did was a negative influence for joining	0%	7%
Incentives offered to join military		
Not offered monetary or non-monetary incentives to join	64%	40%
Offered the ability to "rank-up" as an incentive to join	29%	27%
Offered some type of incentive pay or bonus for joining	7%	27%
Offered small items (e.g., t-shirts, backpacks, mugs) for joining	7%	7%
Assignment of jobs		
Did not get the job they wanted	36%	7%
Happy with job they were assigned	21%	20%
Recruiter made no promises when discussing job assignment	14%	7%
Recommendations to generally improve recruiting		
Minimize wait time or less waiting around	21%	13%
Advertisements and messaging that emphasize the reality of the military and debunk myths perpetuated by Hollywood films	14%	27%
Improve experience at MEPS	7%	47%
Improve recruiting forms, software, or process involving forms and software	0%	27%
More advertising with people in a variety of roles (not just traditional roles)	0%	13%
Recommendations to attract more women		
More female recruiters	79%	13%
More advertising featuring women in a variety of roles	43%	13%
First contact with recruiter		
Recruiting station	86%	87%
School	50%	47%
Online	43%	40%
Mall	0%	7%

Table B.4
Perceptions, Attitudes, and Awareness: Themes from Recruiter Focus Groups and Interviews

Theme	Female Focus Groups	Male Focus Groups
Female recruits' interest in entering combat roles		
Recruiters observed that women were interested in combat MOS	63%	86%
Recruiters observed that women were not interested in combat MOS	63%	29%
Disagreement on whether women were interested in combat MOS	13%	0%
Agreement on whether women want combat MOS	0%	0%
Recruits' general knowledge of the military		
Recruits are informed	50%	29%
Recruits are uninformed	38%	43%
Men and women are equally informed	25%	14%
Women are more informed than men	25%	14%
Agreement on degree to which recruits are informed	0%	29%
Disagreement on degree to which recruits are informed	0%	0%
Recruits' awareness of policy change for women in combat roles		
Aware of policy change before joining	38%	43%
Unaware of policy change	38%	57%
Recruiters' awareness of policy change for women in combat roles		
Aware of policy change	63%	43%
Unaware of policy change	0%	14%
Recruiters' assessment of policy change's impact on recruits' perception of military service		
Policy change had no impact on recruits' perception of the military	13%	0%
Policy change positively affected recruits' perceptions of the military	13%	0%
Recruiters' perspectives on women in combat roles		
Recruiter believes if women can meet standards, they can be in combat	50%	14%
Recruiters do not have opinions on women in combat	25%	14%
If women are in combat, recruiters are concerned that men will stop to help women first	25%	0%
Recruiters disagree on perspectives on women in combat	25%	0%
If women are in combat, recruiters believe that women cannot carry men off the battlefield	13%	0%
Recruiters agree on thoughts on women in combat	0%	14%
Recruiters' perspectives on other services		
Recruiter mentioned perceptions about the Army	25%	43%
Recruiter mentioned perceptions about the Marine Corps	25%	14%
Recruiter mentioned perceptions about the Air Force	25%	14%
Recruiter mentioned perceptions about the Navy	0%	29%

Table B.5
Influences for Joining: Themes from Recruiter Focus Groups and Interviews

Theme	Female Focus Groups	Male Focus Groups
Female recruits' concerns about joining the military		
Sexual harassment/assault is a concern for women	50%	43%
Deployment/war is a concern for women	50%	29%
Physical and weight requirements or physical training are a concern for women	13%	43%
Being away from friends/family is a concern for women	13%	14%
Injury/death is a concern for women	13%	14%
Women do not have concerns when joining	0%	14%
Female recruits' concerns about sexual harassment and assault		
Women are worried about sexual harassment/assault	50%	14%
Women are not worried about sexual harassment/assault	25%	29%
Recruits begin to worry when sexual harassment/assault is mentioned repeatedly during the recruiting process	13%	14%
Recruits were worried about sexual harassment/assault, but learning about the buddy system addresses concerns	13%	14%
Disagreement on whether women are worried about sexual harassment/assault	0%	14%
Recruiters' assessment of policy change's impact on recruiting		
No impact on recruiting	63%	43%
Will affect recruits' job/MOS decisionmaking	13%	0%
Will affect recruiters' recruiting approach	13%	0%
Will affect recruiters' ability to recruit men	13%	0%
Will affect recruiters' ability to recruit women	0%	14%
Influencer support		
Recruiter observed influencers to be supportive	63%	43%
Recruiter observed influencers to be unsupportive	63%	43%
Recruiters had differing perspectives on influencers	13%	0%
Recruiters had similar perspectives on influencers	0%	14%
Influencers' reasons to support joining the military		
Recruiter observed influencers to be supportive of one service over another	25%	57%
Recruiter believed influencers to be supportive because they perceived joining the military to be a good opportunity to do something with your life	25%	0%
Recruiter believed influencers to be supportive because of military career/pay/benefits	25%	0%
Recruiter believed influencers to be supportive because new recruits gain independence	13%	14%
Influencers' reasons to not support joining the military		
Recruiter believed influencers to be unsupportive because of fear of sexual harassment/assault	50%	57%
Recruiter believed influencers to be unsupportive because of fear of sexual harassment/assault	50%	43%
Recruiter believed influencers to be unsupportive because of fear of injury	25%	29%
Recruiter believed influencers to be unsupportive because they had outdated/inaccurate concerns	25%	29%

Table B.6
Recruiting Policies and Strategies: Themes from Recruiter Focus Groups and Interviews

Theme	Female Focus Groups	Male Focus Groups
Where recruiters find recruits		
Schools	100%	86%
Recruits seek out recruiters (e.g., walk in to recruiting station)	38%	57%
Through existing recruits	38%	29%
Malls	25%	14%
Techniques for finding recruits vary by market	13%	43%
Targeting events that are likely to draw applicants with specific skills or interests (e.g., professional school events)	13%	43%
Events (e.g., sports, NASCAR)	0%	43%
Public (e.g., school) lists	0%	14%
Recruitment training		
Took official recruiting introductory course	88%	100%
Believe training was not enough	38%	29%
Mentored/shadowed other recruiters as part of training	25%	43%
Learned recruiting individually on the job	25%	43%
Recruiter used or produced shared training resources	25%	14%
Received materials (e.g., books) as training tools	13%	29%
Received other additional recruiting training	0%	14%
Recruiting targets and incentives		
Recruiter has targets for MOS/job specialties	63%	71%
Recruiter has to meet targets for qualifications (e.g., high test scores, ASVAB, degree)	50%	29%
Recruiter has to meet gender targets	38%	43%
Recruiter has to meet targets for reserves	38%	43%
Recruiter receives individual incentives for reaching goals	38%	29%
Recruiters incentives have changed	38%	29%
Recruiter has to meet team recruiting goals	38%	14%
Recruiter has to meet an overall target number/goal	38%	14%
Recruiter has to meet individual recruiting goals	25%	14%
Recruiter has team incentives for reaching goals	25%	0%
Recruiting tools		
Recruiters are able to offer higher pay or bonus as incentive to join	50%	29%
Recruiters are able to offer little gifts (e.g., t-shirts) as incentive to join	25%	0%
Recruiter does not offer additional incentives to join	0%	14%
Recruiting best practices		
Recruiter aims to sell the service, not the job	63%	71%
Recruiter believes transparency/honesty is an effective recruiting practice	50%	57%

Table B.6—Continued

Theme	Female Focus Groups	Male Focus Groups
Recruiter tries to relate to the new recruits through culture (language) or hobbies (sports)	38%	43%
Recruiter finds "gaps" in new recruit's life and explains how the military can help	38%	43%
Recruiter believes it is important to always be available and to get back to potential recruits quickly	38%	14%
Recruiter believes using personal experience an effective recruiting practice	25%	43%
Recruiter believes strategies for identifying recruits vary by market	25%	29%
Recruiter aims to sell a specific job	13%	14%
Recruiters generally agreed upon effective techniques/strategies for identifying recruits	0%	29%
Recruiters disagreed about effective techniques/strategies for identifying recruits	0%	14%
Recruiters' best practices for recruiting women		
Referring a recruit to a female recruiter is an effective way to recruit women	50%	43%
Responding to or creating resources pertaining to female-specific questions is an effective way to recruit women	38%	0%
Emphasizing family-friendly policies is an effective way to recruit women	25%	0%
Recruiters' ways of addressing recruits' concerns of sexual harassment and assault		
Emphasize rates of sexual harassment/assault in civilian society	63%	0%
Use personal experience	38%	0%
Emphasize recruits' personal responsibility/behavior	38%	0%
Emphasize reality	13%	14%
Recruiters' ways of addressing influencers' concerns of sexual harassment and assault		
Emphasize reality of military life	25%	29%
Use personal experience	25%	14%
Emphasize protocols/trainings/structure	13%	29%
Emphasize recruits' personal responsibility/behavior	13%	0%
Recruiters try to specifically recruit women		
Recruiters try specifically to recruit women	38%	43%
Recruiters do not try specifically to recruit women	25%	43%
Recruiter incentives for recruiting women		
There are incentives for recruiting women	13%	0%
There are disincentives for recruiting women (e.g., looking like a sexual predator)	13%	43%
Recruiters agree on whether they specifically recruit women	13%	29%
Recruiter approaches to recruiting women		
Use same approach for recruiting men as recruiting women	75%	57%
Use different approach for recruiting men and women	63%	29%
Recruiters agree on approaches to recruiting men and women	0%	14%
Recruiters disagree on approaches to recruiting men and women	0%	0%
Percentage of potential female recruits		
Less than 20%	38%	29%

Table B.6—Continued

Theme	Female Focus Groups	Male Focus Groups
Between 20–50%	25%	29%
More than 50%	0%	0%
Percentage of female recruits that eventually join military		
Of potential female recruits, less than 20% sign	13%	14%
Of potential female recruits, more than 50% sign	13%	0%
Of potential female recruits, between 20–50% sign	0%	43%
Recommendations to generally improve recruiting		
Improved job selection/information	25%	29%
More advertising	13%	71%
Improving software/recruiting processes	13%	57%
Modifying goals	13%	29%
More advertising of a variety of roles	13%	14%
Improved access to schools	13%	0%
Less paperwork/fewer requirements	0%	43%
Fewer external obligations or fewer responsibilities unrelated to recruiting	0%	29%
Recommendations to attract more women		
More advertising of women in a variety of jobs	50%	14%
Recruiter incentives specifically for recruiting women	25%	14%
More family friendly policies	25%	14%
More female recruiters	13%	29%
More advertising	0%	29%
Recruiting experience		
Fewer than two years of experience recruiting	63%	57%
2–5 years of experience recruiting	63%	57%
Did not have previous experience recruiting	25%	29%
Five or more years of experience recruiting	0%	57%
Have had previous experience recruiting	0%	29%
Entry into recruiting		
Requested (or volunteered for) recruiting position	75%	57%
Position was assigned/involuntary	50%	57%

References

Aspin, Les, "Direct Ground Combat Definition and Assignment Rule," Washington, D.C.: Office of the Secretary of Defense, January 13, 1994.

Berkowitz, Susan G., Mary Achatz, and Shelly Perry Westat, *Career Plans and Military Propensity of Young Women: Interviews with 1997 Youth Attitude Tracking Study Respondents*, DMDC Report No. 2000-01, May 1999.

Corbett, Sara, "The Women's War," *New York Times Magazine*, March 18, 2007. As of May 8, 2017: http://www.nytimes.com/2007/03/18/magazine/18cover.html

Defense Advisory Committee on Women in the Services (DACOWITS), *Quarterly Meeting Minutes*, September 18–19, 2014.

Defense Manpower Data Center, Human Resources Strategic Assessment Program, *2012 Workplace and Gender Relations Survey of Active Duty Members: Tabulations of Responses*, DMDC Report No. 2012-065, April 2013.

Ford, Michael T., Jennifer L. Gibson, Brian K. Griepentrog, and Sean M. Marsh, "Reassessing the Association of Intent to Join the Military and Subsequent Enlistment," *Military Psychology*, Vol. 26, No. 1, 2014, pp. 1–14.

Joint Advertising, Market Research, and Studies, "Women in Combat: Potential Impact on Recruiting," executive note, January 2013.

Kilpatrick, Dean G., Heidi S. Resnick, Kenneth J. Ruggiero, Lauren M. Conoscenti, and Jenna Mccauley, *Drug-Facilitated, Incapacitated, and Forcible Rape: A National Study*, Charleston, S.C.: Medical University of South Carolina, National Crime Victims Research and Treatment Center, 2007. As of May 4, 2016: https://www.ncjrs.gov/pdffiles1/nij/grants/219181.pdf

Morral, Andrew R., Kristie L. Gore, Terry L. Schell, Barbara Bicksler, Coreen Farris, Bonnie Ghosh-Dastidar, Lisa H. Jaycox, Dean Kilpatrick, Stephan Kistler, Amy Street, Terri Tanielian and Kayla M. Williams, *Sexual Assault and Sexual Harassment in the U.S. Military: Volume 1. Design of the 2014 RAND Military Workplace Study*, Santa Monica, Calif.: RAND Corporation, RR-870/1-OSD, 2014. As of March 16, 2016: http://www.rand.org/pubs/research_reports/RR870z1.html

Office of National Drug Control Policy, "Report to the White House Council on Women and Girls," 2010. As of May 8, 2017:
https://www.hsdl.org/?view&did=24166

Panetta, Leon E, "Elimination of the 1994 Direct Ground Combat Definition and Assignment Rule," Washington, D.C.: Office of the Secretary of Defense, January 24, 2013.

Patten, Eileen, and Kim Parker, *Women in the US Military: Growing Share, Distinctive Profile*, Washington, D.C.: Pew Research Center, 2011.

Secretary of the Air Force Memorandum to the Secretary of Defense, "Air Force Implementation Plan for Integrating Women into Career Fields Engaged in Direct Ground Combat," Washington, D.C., April 24, 2014.

United States Code, Title 10, Section 513, Enlistments: Delayed Entry Program, January 3, 2012.